DINNER
·FOR DOGS·

THE EXPERIMENT

BECAUSE EVERY BOOK IS A TEST OF NEW IDEAS

To my family
Kim, Holly and Lily

DINNER
· FOR DOGS ·

· 50 HOME-COOKED RECIPES FOR A HAPPY, HEALTHY DOG ·

HENRIETTA MORRISON

THE EXPERIMENT
NEW YORK

DINNER FOR DOGS: *50 Home-Cooked Recipes for a Happy, Healthy Dog*

Text © 2012, 2013 Henrietta Morrison
Cover and p. 8 photograph copyright © 2012 Vicki Couchman

First published in the United Kingdom in 2012 by Ebury Press, an imprint of Ebury Publishing,
a Random House Group company.

The Experiment, LLC
260 Fifth Avenue
New York, NY 10001-6408
theexperimentpublishing.com

This book contains the opinions and ideas of its author. It is intended to provide helpful and informative material on the subjects addressed in the book. It is sold with the understanding that the author and publisher are not engaged in rendering medical, health, or any other kind of personal professional services in the book. The author and publisher specifically disclaim all responsibility for any liability, loss, or risk—personal or otherwise—that is incurred as a consequence, directly or indirectly, of the use and application of any of the contents of this book.

The Experiment's books are available at special discounts when purchased in bulk for premiums and sales promotions as well as for fundraising or educational use. For details, contact us at info@theexperimentpublishing.com.

Library of Congress Cataloging-in-Publication Data

Morrison, Henrietta.
Dinner for dogs : 50 home-cooked recipes for a happy, healthy dog / Henrietta Morrison.
pages cm
Includes index.
ISBN 978-1-61519-084-3 (paper or cloth) -- ISBN 978-1-61519-176-5 (ebook) 1. Dogs--Food--Recipes. I. Title.
SF427.4.M674 2013
636.7'083--dc23
2012040087

ISBN 978-1-61519-084-3
Ebook ISBN 978-1-61519-176-5

Author photograph by Vicki Couchman
Project editor: Anne McDowall
Design and illustrations: Mad River
Typesetting by Pauline Neuwirth, Neuwirth & Associates, Inc.

Manufactured in China
Distributed by Workman Publishing Company, Inc.
Distributed simultaneously in Canada by Thomas Allen and Son Ltd.
First North American edition published June 2013
10 9 8 7 6 5 4 3 2 1

Contents

·Introduction·

The only question in life that really matters to dogs is: "What's for dinner?" As pet owners, we feel a deep-down satisfaction when we see our dogs tucking into their food. Luckily, feeding time in our house is a moment of much excitement and anticipation.

If your dog stops eating his or her food, it's usually a sign that something's up. I know how concerning this can be: When my dog Lily was a year old, she stopped eating altogether. She would run up to her bowl with her usual exuberance and then back away slowly. I was horrified! I tried different foods, but to no avail; she would seem enthusiastic until she smelled what was in the bowl and would then turn away and wander off, looking rather dejected. I started cooking her chicken, rice, vegetables and apples, which I knew she loved, and she began to eat properly again. This was definitely good news all around, and I kept a copy of the recipes I made.

Cooking for your pet is easy, satisfying and a great way to bond! It is good to know that what you have prepared is a nourishing, yummy meal of real food rather than the processed grease-laden dry pellets or chunk-and-jelly that are generally sold in stores.

LILY

Healthy eating for dogs

The philosophy behind each recipe in this book is Hippocrates' holistic mantra "Let Food Be Thy Medicine and Medicine Thy Food." In other words, eating well will contribute to your good health, and eating badly will be detrimental.

The same goes for our pets. If it's not good enough for me, it's not good enough for Lily. That's not to say Lily should eat what I eat (too many croissants would be on the list!), but if I'm not prepared to eat it, then I don't feed it to my dog.

Ready-made versus home-cooked

Providing food for your dog is your responsibility as a pet owner. There are several ways of doing this: You can roll up your sleeves and get cooking, buy a really good ready-made food or try a combination of both.

It's always been a tricky thing to know what to feed your dog. A pretty assertive lobby from pet food manufacturers warns you not to cook for your pet under any circumstances because you may not be feeding your pet properly or, worse, may be making them ill.

I think a clear distinction needs to be made between cooking for your pet, which is an extremely rewarding and caring thing to do, and giving your pet leftover scraps of pizza and other takeout, which have little nutritional value to your dog.

It's also good to give your dog a varied diet so they benefit from the whole spectrum of nutrients. You'll find more on the "building blocks" of a healthy diet for your pet on pages 12–23.

> " If it's not good enough for me, it's not good enough for Lily. . . . If I'm not prepared to eat it, then I don't feed it to my dog. "

Raw Food

I am often asked about raw food. I'm not an advocate, as I'm concerned about the parasites in raw food and the stories I hear of how raw food has made some dogs very ill. Raw food advocates put forward the argument that your dog is healthier and looks better when fed raw food. For me this is not the case—what is important is that you feed your dog good food. Whether it is cooked or not is not the point. Interestingly, Harvard recently published a study showing that cooking food for mammals makes the food much easier to digest and metabolize than raw food.

The problem with "pet food"

Buying food for your pet is a bit like entering a minefield. In most supermarkets, pet food is in the same aisle as laundry products. This is because pet food has been viewed as a commodity, just like detergent. Supermarkets bulk buy at the cheapest prices, and it's a market that is almost solely controlled by multinational corporations that are experts at producing millions of cans of dog food an hour.

But in my opinion, food for your dog should be just that—real food made from ingredients you or I would recognize immediately. One of the things that has amazed me is that we owners don't trust our instincts when we are buying food for our pets. Even though the food may smell awful and contain all sorts of horrible things, we carry on buying it and feeding it to our dogs.

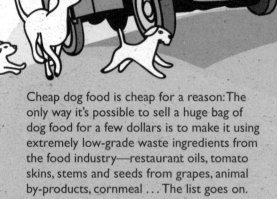

Cheap dog food is cheap for a reason: The only way it's possible to sell a huge bag of dog food for a few dollars is to make it using extremely low-grade waste ingredients from the food industry—restaurant oils, tomato skins, stems and seeds from grapes, animal by-products, cornmeal . . . The list goes on.

You'll find more information on how to read a dog food label to help you navigate your way through all the pet foods on the market on pages 24–27.

Using the recipes in this book

The recipes in this book are designed to be easy, healthy and low fat. There is no added salt and most of the recipes are gluten-free. You will find here a selection of everyday meals and treats, as well as recipes suitable for old dogs and those that have been unwell.

They do not claim to be complete meals as we would then have to get very technical about adding in enough calcium, making sure there's not too much copper, etc. A wide range of vitamins are added to complete pet foods to make sure they provide the full spectrum of nutrition. Your vet is the best person to talk to about nutrition for your particular dog to determine how to best provide your dog a complete meal.

I've included some nutritional information as a guide to what's in the recipe. These have been calculated on an "as fed" basis—this means that you get the nutritional value of the cooked food. This will give you some guidelines on calorie counts and how much fat and protein they provide. Note that the protein and fat percentages given refer to the percentage (by weight) of each dish made up of protein or fat.

All of the recipes in this book can be made ahead and stored to make mealtime easy. My advice would be to try to make the time to prepare a home-cooked meal for your dog at least once a week. If you have time for more, great, and if not, then make sure that on the other days you are feeding your dog a really good pet food. Don't go for the cheapest option; buy the best food you can—your dog is worth it!

Remember: Your dog depends on you alone for food and nourishment—indeed for survival. Lily is so excited to see me every morning! I know she loves me, but I also know she's excited because it means breakfast is on its way!

I hope you have fun cooking these delicious recipes from Lily's Kitchen.

Henrietta

• Top Tip •

Cooking for your dog is easy: It takes a bit more time than opening a can, but you can make the food in batches and either refrigerate or freeze it. For those recipes that store well, you'll find specific instructions within each recipe.

The building blocks of a healthy diet

If you are planning to cook for your dog on a fairly regular basis it is important that you provide a balanced diet of proteins, fats and carbohydrates. Complete dog food contains all these elements as well as the necessary vitamins, amino acids and minerals, such as calcium, that are important to keep your dog in good health. It's also good to provide a variety of ingredients so that your dog gets the whole spectrum of nutrition available from a wide range of ingredients. I do rather feel sorry for the poor fellow who has to eat the same brand of dry kibble forever. It would be a bit like us eating buttered toast for every meal forever—it might keep us alive but it wouldn't keep us in peak health.

Proteins

Proteins are essential for your dog for good muscle and healthy tissue growth. Animal proteins—found in meat, fish, poultry, eggs and some dairy products—are the easiest for your dog to digest and make the best use of. Proteins from plant sources are harder to digest and do not contain the full range of essential amino acids that dogs need. However, you can combine animal and plant proteins together and include beans, peas and lentils for their protein content.

Meat is a rich source of protein, minerals and vitamins. It is, however, low in calcium and relatively high in phosphorus. If you are cooking for your dog regularly—say, more than three times a week—you will need to add a calcium source such as raw meaty bones to his or her daily rations in order to ensure a healthy level of these two important minerals. Fatty meat is actually good for dogs: If they eat only lean meat, they will be missing out on some key vitamins (see opposite).

Remember to include organ meat, too, as this includes a critical array of nutrients not found in muscle meat. Liver and kidneys are a rich source of vitamins, especially vitamin A and minerals. The recipes here are made with a range of different proteins, including chicken, turkey, fish, beef and lamb. Variety, as in all parts of a balanced diet, is the key, so try cooking different sources of protein for your dog. Bland, white meat, such as chicken, is easier to digest and hence a good choice for a convalescent dog.

Feeding your dog twice a day rather than once makes it easier for him or her to digest food properly. And it means your dog will look forward to something twice a day rather than once—double happiness!

Fats— for energy

Dogs love the taste of fat, especially animal fat. You'll notice there's always a very willing eater of leftover fat from a juicy steak! Fats are a very important part of your pet's diet. Fats act as a carrier for the important fat-soluble vitamins, such as Vitamins A, D, E and K.

However, it's really important to strike a balance between feeding your dog enough fat for good health, but not so much that your lovely lean dog turns into a bit of a heavyweight. An overweight dog is prone to other serious health problems, such as pancreatitis. Fat contains twice as many calories as protein or carbohydrates.

Essential fatty acids (EFAs) play an important role and are crucial to your dog's health. Dogs need to have these added to their diet as they cannot make them themselves. EFAs are crucial to every cell in your dog's body and aid in the regulation of nearly every bodily function. They play a key role in helping to regulate the immune system and can act as powerful anti-inflammatories. They are also particularly important for maintaining a healthy skin and coat, for brain and kidney function and for a healthy heart. The most important families of fatty acids are the omega-3s and the omega-6s.

Omega-6 (also known as linoleic acid) is found in ingredients such as sunflower oil.

It plays an important role in skin health, tissue repair and in providing a healthy immune system. However, too much omega-6 can cause skin allergies and other problems.

Most diets already contain enough omega-6, so concentrate on making sure your dog gets enough omega-3 fatty acids.

The richest sources of omega-3 are fish, particularly cold-water, oily fish such as salmon, herring, mackerel, anchovies and sardines, all of which are good to feed your dog. These are all full of docosahexaenoic acid (DHA) and eicosapentaenoic acid (EPA), which are the chemical names for the omega-3s. There is also a type of omega-3, alpha-linolenic acid (ALA), that is found in plants, most importantly in flaxseed oil and hempseed oil.

If you are considering giving your dog omega-3 or omega-6 supplements, please discuss it with your vet first, because too much can cause a variety of health problems and suppress the immune system.

Although commonly given, cod liver oil is not a beneficial supplement for your dog. It contains high levels of vitamins A and D, which if given daily can build up and cause toxicity. For cooking purposes, I generally use canola oil or olive oil, which are more resistant to the damaging effects of heat than other vegetable oils. Try to stick to a rough guide of one tablespoon of oil for your dog per day—halve this amount if you have a small dog.

> **EFAs are important for maintaining a healthy skin and coat, for brain and kidney function and for a healthy heart.**

Carbohydrates

These are very important as they supply the fuel for activity as well as provide fiber, which helps the gastrointestinal tract to function happily. Good sources of fiber include oats, brown rice, potato and whole wheat. Vegetables and fruit also provide carbohydrates. Grains are basic energy foods—they are a source of complex carbohydrates. Many commercial dog foods have a very high level of grains.

Dogs benefit from having a low amount of grain in their diet—up to 30 percent is fine. By using a few well-selected whole grains in the recipes you cook, you will provide your dog with the benefits of slow-release (low GI) carbohydrates, fiber and a wide range of important vitamins and minerals (notably vitamin E and B complex). In addition to providing energy, carbohydrates maintain the health of the thyroid, liver, heart, brain and nervous tissue.

On the following pages you will find an introduction to some of the key cereal grains available for use in recipes for your dog; choose different ones for their particular qualities.

• Top Tip •

It's become rather fashionable when feeding your dog to avoid carbs. When carbs are made from whole vegetable and grain sources, they are definitely a good thing, in moderation. It's important to consider what percentage of the overall meal they make up—I think up to 35 percent is fine for a daily meal. Unfortunately lots of store-bought dog foods contain far too many low quality carbs and grains, as these are usually cheap by-products of the agrochemical industry.

Introducing grains

Barley

This is the mildest and least irritating of all the cereals and therefore often used for feeding dogs that are unwell. Pearled barley has had the inedible outer hulls removed. Barley has low gluten content, a mild, sweet flavor and a pleasing, chewy texture. It helps to nourish and soothe the entire gastro-intestinal tract. Barley is highly nutritious and good for underweight dogs that need building up.

Buckwheat*

A power-packed grain, buckwheat is special in that it contains many essential amino acids as well as a substance called rutin that helps strengthen the capillaries and aids the circulation. It is an excellent grain for cold weather months because of the warming and drying effects on the body. It has a reputation of being a good blood builder and neutralizer of toxic wastes. This is a gluten-free grain with a sweet flavor. It cleanses the intestines and improves appetite.

· Gluten Intolerance ·

Just as many people are gluten intolerant, so are a growing number of dogs. Gluten is a combination of two proteins found in many grains, but highest in wheat. (Gluten is what causes bread to rise—when the dough is kneaded, gluten traps the carbon dioxide released by the yeast.) The following grains are gluten-free: amaranth, buckwheat, corn, millet, quinoa and rice.

*denotes gluten-free

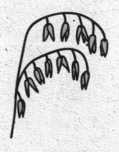

Corn*

The most widely grown crop worldwide, with a large percentage now genetically modified, corn can be used as a grain, an oil or a flour (cornmeal). It is a gluten-free grain with a sweet flavor. However, although most commercial dog foods, particularly in the US, are made with a huge amount of corn, many dogs find corn quite hard to digest, so I haven't included corn in any of the recipes in this book.

Millet*

Exceedingly nutritious, millet contains an abundance of minerals and vitamins and the most complete protein of any of the cereal grains. Millet is one of the least allergenic foods, so good for dogs with a sensitive digestion.

Oats

Great for maintaining energy and warmth during the cold winter months because they contain more fat and protein than most other grains, oats are an adaptogen, meaning they improve the body's resistance to stress and help keep the system in a healthy state of balance. Oats support the nervous system and help regulate the thyroid gland. Like all whole grains, oats have a mild laxative effect as they are high in fiber.

Quinoa*

Pronounced *keen-wah*, quinoa was a principal grain of the Incas, given sacred status as a "mother grain." Because it is calorie and protein rich, quinoa is a particularly valuable grain for convalescing dogs, as well as for those that have a sensitive digestive system. Quinoa contains a balanced set of essential amino acids (including lysine, which is missing or low in many cereal grains), making it the most complete protein source among plant foods. It is also a good source of fiber and phosphorus and is high in magnesium and iron. In fact, quinoa is such a "superfood" that NASA is considering using it as a food for astronauts!

Rice*

A staple grain for more than half of the world's population (the Chinese word for rice means "grain of life"), rice is a sweet, neutral grain that is often recommended as part of the diet in convalescence because it helps to soothe the stomach and expel toxins from the system. Rice is said to calm the nervous system, relieve depression and strengthen the internal organs. Whole grain rice is a source of B vitamins.

Rye

Closely related to barley and wheat but with a lower gluten content, rye has a strong flavor and is a versatile grain that can be combined with others. Rye is said to build strong muscles, promote energy and endurance and aid nail, fur and bone formation. It benefits the liver and is a filling grain that is high in soluble fiber.

Spelt

Believed to be among the most ancient of cultivated cereals, this type of wheat was highly favored by the Romans. Spelt has a very low allergenic profile, so it is suitable for gluten-intolerant dogs. Its high water solubility makes spelt very easily absorbed in the body and hence easily digested. Because it is not a hybridized grain like wheat, it is generally higher in protein, vitamins and minerals.

Wheat

Wheat is said to have a calming effect on the mind. Wheat allergy may be linked to the huge quantity that is eaten, as well as to the highly refined state it is now in, since few individuals have allergies to the heirloom varieties of wheat such as kamut and spelt. Whole wheat is the most nutritious form of wheat; refined wheat has lost as much as 80 percent of its vitamins and minerals and 93 percent of its fiber. Wheat bran (the outer fibrous layers of the grain) is typically added to provide bulk and fiber to the diet, good for treating constipation. Wheat germ is nutritionally the best part of the grain and contains the entire vitamin B complex.

• Buying & Cooking Grains •

- Buy whole grains as they have greater nutritional benefits; whole grain rice is a good starting point.
- Always rinse grains well before use to remove any coating or debris.
- Soaking grains overnight before cooking helps to increase digestibility and nutritional value. (You can then cook the grains in this nutrient-rich water.)

Vegetables

About 20 to 30 percent of your dog's diet should consist of fresh vegetables. Lightly steaming or cooking them makes them easier to digest. In addition to being full of antioxidants and other phytonutrients, vegetables are an important source of minerals, vitamins and fiber in the diet.

The following are all good vegetables to feed your dog.

Broccoli

A good summer vegetable that brightens the eyes and is helpful for eye inflammation, broccoli contains abundant pantothenic acid and vitamin A, which benefit the skin. It contains more vitamin C than citrus fruits and is a high natural source of sulphur, iron and B vitamins. (Avoid in cases of thyroid deficiency.)

Butternut squash

Winter squash (including the butternut variety) contains greater amounts of natural sugars, carbohydrates and vitamin A than summer squash. Butternut squash has anti-inflammatory properties and is said to help get rid of intestinal parasites such as worms.

Cabbage

Green and red cabbage improves digestion and circulation and is good for treating constipation. Cabbage contains iodine and is a rich source of vitamin C (it contains more than oranges). Vitamin E is concentrated in the outer leaves, which also contain at least a third more calcium than the inner ones.

Carrot

Carrots contain one of the richest sources of the antioxidant beta-carotene (provitamin A), which is said to protect against cancer. Beta-carotene and vitamin A benefit the skin and are anti-inflammatory for the intestinal lining.

· Top Tips ·

- Use vegetables that are in season.
- Wash vegetables before using them.
- Steam or only lightly cook them—too much cooking can lead to loss of nutrients.
- Add the nutrient-rich cooking water to the food.
- Include vegetables of a variety of colors, as they contain different phytonutrients and antioxidants.
- If using raw vegetables, purée or liquidize them before use so your dog can eat them without any chewing issues.

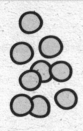

Lentils

Lentils are a good source of soluble, digestible protein. They have diuretic properties and are beneficial to the heart and circulation. They stimulate the adrenal system and increase the vitality of the kidneys.

Parsnips

Even richer in vitamins and minerals than carrots, parsnips are high in potassium and a great source of good-quality dietary fiber.

Peas

Peas assist with digestion, are diuretic and mildly laxative (good for treating constipation) and are also used to counteract spasms.

Spinach

Spinach has diuretic properties and a laxative effect. The rich iron and chlorophyll content of spinach builds blood. It also contains high levels of vitamin A.

Fruit

Fruit contains valuable minerals, vitamins, enzymes and fiber, and it is easily digested. The alkaline element in fruit combined with its acids stimulates the liver and pancreas, providing a natural laxative action.

Many dogs enjoy fruits as a snack or as a regular part of their diet. Try out some of the following fruits with your dog to see which he or she prefers. Blueberries, apples and papaya are Lily's favorites! Fresh is best, but frozen is fine too.

Apples

Apples stimulate the appetite and remedy indigestion. This ability is due in part to the presence of malic and tartaric acids, which inhibit the growth of disease-producing bacteria in the digestive tracts. Apples contain pectin, which helps detoxify the body from the effects of everyday pollution. Apples and their juice are also cleansing and beneficial for the liver and gall bladder.

Bananas

A nutritional powerhouse, bananas are a rich source of potassium, which benefits the nervous and muscular systems (no wonder tennis players eat them during matches!). They have a soothing effect on the gastrointestinal system, so are especially useful for stomach ulcers, and they are said to help promote sleep. Always wait until they are fully ripe before using.

Blueberries

Known for their very high antioxidant content and antiaging properties, blueberries contain anthocyanins, which have anti-inflammatory and anti-cancer properties. Blueberries are also good for the brain—new research in people shows that blueberries may help to slow signs of cognitive decline (Alzheimers).

Melon

An excellent cleanser and rehydrator, melon is a good fruit to use in the summer months. (Remove the seeds before using.)

Water

We all know that it's important to drink plenty of water every day, and the same is true for our dogs. Water keeps your dog well hydrated and helps to make sure his or her kidneys are regularly flushed out. Change the water in your dog's bowl at least once a day. Lily is especially fussy about this!

Oranges

Oranges aid digestion and help alleviate trapped gas. They are an excellent source of vitamin C (when used fresh), which benefits the immune system.

Papaya

An extremely nutrient-dense fruit, especially rich in vitamins A and C as well as potassium, calcium, phosphorus and iron, papaya cleanses the digestive tract, eliminating indigestion, reducing gas, soothing inflammation and cleansing and detoxifying the whole body. Papaya is good for dogs recovering from any digestive upset.

Raspberries

Of benefit to the liver and kidneys, enriching and cleansing the blood of toxins, raspberries help control urinary function and are said to help relieve excessive and frequent urination, especially at night. They are also reputed to help improve vision.

Strawberries

Rich in silica and vitamin C, strawberries are useful for connective tissue and blood vessel repair. They also improve appetite and are said to help relieve urinary difficulties.

How to read a dog food label

It's handy to know what to look out for when you are looking for a ready-made food for your dog. Price is generally a good indicator: If a food is cheap, it's because it's made with cheap ingredients. Buying the best you can afford for your dog will be worth it in the long term—their health and happiness depend on it!

Dry foods

Dry foods were invented as a way of getting rid of waste material that food factories produced. Dry foods usually have a very pungent smell because they have had so many flavorings and fats added to encourage your dog to eat them.

All dry foods are not the same and you really do get what you pay for. More expensive dry foods made with whole ingredients include a wide variety of ingredients and chelated minerals, which your dog will be able to absorb better, rather than chemical compounds that do not get properly absorbed and just pass through the body.

Here's an indication of what those ingredients on the label actually mean, so that you can navigate your way through the pet food aisle and choose exactly the kind of food you want your dog to eat.

> **Buying the best you can afford for your dog will be worth it in the long run.**

Chicken by-product meal/powdered chicken/dry chicken/cooked chicken

These are all descriptions for an ingredient that is used in almost every dry food on the market today. Chicken by-product meal is made by boiling chicken by-products such as carcass, skin and feathers, siphoning off the fat to make tallow, and drying what is left at a very high temperature, then grinding it into a fine powder resembling dark sand. It produces a high level of protein, but dogs have trouble digesting it. This together with poor ingredients is what makes your dog gassy. Chicken and other meat meal is preserved with very heavy-duty artificial preservatives. When you are looking for a really good dry food, look for one that has fresh meat, rather than meat meal, listed as the first ingredient.

• No Substitute For Brushing! •

Some vets will tell you that dogs must eat only dry food to clean their teeth and prevent dental disease. But this alone won't ensure clean teeth. If you speak to the veterinary technician, he or she will tell you that the only thing that really keeps your dog's teeth clean is regular brushing!

Ash

The percentage of ash provides a helpful indicator of the quality of the dry food you are buying. The lower the ash content, the better: Look for a dry food that has between 3 and 4 percent. Any dry food that contains more than 5 percent ash will have a lot of chicken by-product meal in it (see page 25). More than 8 percent ash is a worrying amount.

Tomato pomace

This is simply tomato skins, which, as any nutritionist will tell you, are made of indigestible fibers.

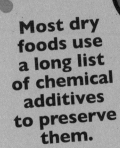

> **Most dry foods use a long list of chemical additives to preserve them.**

Oils and fats

Dogs love fat! It's cheap and it's tasty—and it's the only thing that tastes good to them in a kibble. Fat is sprayed onto the outside of the kibble to encourage dogs to eat up. Some dogs have figured this out and just lick the outside. Around an 8 to 10 percent fat content is healthy; dry foods containing more than 12 percent should be avoided.

Additives

Most dry foods use a long list of chemical additives to preserve them. The worst offenders are the semimoist dry foods, which contain lots of preservatives to stop the moist pieces from getting moldy. The statement "No added preservatives, colors or flavorings" on a label may, in fact, be meaningless, as only the ingredients added during manufacturing legally have to be declared, not the preservatives that have been added to these ingredients before they arrive in the factory!

• Top Tip •

Never feed your dog cooked bones as they are likely to splinter and get stuck in his or her throat. Choose big raw bones and submerge them in boiling water for a minute to kill off the surface bacteria. Never leave your dog unsupervised with a bone.

Wet foods

Choose a food with lots of whole ingredients—pieces of food that you can recognize—chunks of real meat and real vegetables. Ideally, you want a food that resembles something you would make at home but that is also a complete food, i.e., with the precise balance of ingredients and nutrients your dog needs.

Most wet foods are made either as a "chunk and jelly" or as a "chunk and gravy." When I first fed Lily wet food, I thought that the chunks in wet food were in fact pieces of meat; actually, they had no meat in them at all! What are made to look like chunks of meat are often in fact waste products and flour that have been formed into chunks. The best way to identify the chunks is to pull one out from the food and squeeze it to see if you are left with a powdery mush or a real piece of meat.

The "gravy" or "jelly" is usually a highly flavored water-based fluid that usually contains a wide variety of additives and sweeteners to entice your dog to eat it.

Calorie requirements for an active dog

It's handy to have a rough idea of how many calories your dog needs every day, although this varies between dogs depending on their metabolism and energy requirements. You need to take age into account, too: Old dogs generally need up to 20 percent less food than younger ones.

You are the best judge of how much to feed your pet. Weighing your dog every month or so will enable you to keep an eye on any weight gain or loss and to decrease or increase the amount of food accordingly. It's also a good idea to get an objective view: We tend to look at our pets adoringly and may not notice if they are a little overweight! Ask your vet what weight your dog should be maintaining.

The table below gives an estimate of how many calories your dog needs on a daily basis. An active dog is a dog who goes out happily for a couple of hours walking and running per day. A resting dog is one that is not so keen on walking and is probably elderly. The more exercise a dog does, the more calories he or she needs.

Weight lb (kg)	Active calories	Resting calories
11 (5)	374	234
13 (6)	429	268
15½ (7)	481	301
17½ (8)	532	332
19¾ (9)	581	363
22 (10)	629	393
24¼ (11)	676	422
26½ (12)	722	451
28¾ (13)	766	479
30¾ (14)	810	506
33 (15)	853	533
35¼ (16)	896	560
37½ (17)	937	586
39¾ (18)	978	611
42 (19)	1012	637
44 (20)	1059	662
46¼ (21)	1098	686
48½ (22)	1137	711
50¾ (23)	1176	735
53 (24)	1214	759
55 (25)	1252	782

what not to feed your dog

Here is a list of things your dog should not eat. If for some reason, he or she does get hold of any of these items and eat them, call your vet for advice on what to do.

Alcohol

Alcohol has a very toxic effect on dogs and can make them very sick.

Artificial sweeteners

They are easy to forget about, but artificial sweeteners can have an immediately fatal effect on dogs. A lady once phoned me in tears: Her dog had died because she had given him the rest of her cereal to finish and she had sweetened it with artificial sweetener.

Avocado

Avocados are very high in fat and can cause digestive problems in dogs. They contain a chemical that can be toxic to some dogs and harm their liver, heart and lungs.

Chocolate

Even 2 ounces (50 g) of chocolate can be fatal for a dog because it contains an ingredient called theobromide, which is incredibly toxic to dogs. It will be a slow and painful death, too, so if you suspect your dog has had chocolate, you need to take him or her immediately to the vet to be given an antidote.

Coffee

Caffeine is harmful for dogs and can cause seizures. (Chocolate-covered espresso beans are particularly toxic for dogs.)

Grapes and raisins

A particular mold that can grow on grapes is very harmful to dogs and can prove fatal.

Onions

Another food to avoid, onions can cause anemia in dogs.

· Top Tip ·

Make sure that you core all apples and remove stones and seeds from fruit such as apples, plums, peaches and cherries before feeding these fruits to your dog.

Puppy power!

> "Puppies need to eat several times a day due to their small stomachs."

It was wonderful to watch Lily with her puppies, instinctively knowing what to do—no training needed at all! Her children are now four years old and the picture of health.

Many owners give their new puppies food that has been given to them by the breeder or by the shelter they have adopted them from. Do your research! Observe your dog and see how he or she is doing on his or her current food. If you think your dog needs better quality food, then have the confidence to switch foods. If you notice your dog has greasy skin, fur that smells, lots of wind and any itchiness, these are the first clues that the food your dog is on is probably not the best for him or her.

Puppies need to eat several times a day, as they have small stomachs and need lots of nutrition. Ideally pups that are four months old should be fed four times a day, then three times a day until they are six months old. After that, you can begin to feed them twice a day like an adult dog. Puppies should grow at the appropriate rate for their breed—not too quickly and not too slowly.

The recipes in this book can be used for puppies, but only alongside a specific diet that has been formulated especially for puppies. Pups need a balanced diet that includes appropriate amounts of calcium to ensure good bone formation. This diet is best provided by a veterinary nutritionist until they are six months old.

The treats in this book are perfect for puppies, as they don't contain the usual array of hidden preservatives and additives. They are naturally delicious and nutritious and will be invaluable in training your puppy to have good habits and get rid of the bad ones!

Poop!

Your dog's poop is a very important issue—it's your daily indicator of how your dog is doing and whether he or she is digesting food well. In addition, of course, you need your dog's poop to be easy to pick up—that means nice and firm.

Many dog owners are nervous about straying from a complete dry food diet because they are worried the poop will be too soft. Well, the good news is that a good-quality wet food or homemade food is made with whole ingredients that have been properly digested, so what comes out is easy to pick up because it's the waste and fiber rather than what seems like the same weight of ingredients that went into the bowl in the first place.

When you feed your dog a low-quality food, your dog produces rather a lot of poop! Many ingredients in commercial pet foods cannot be broken down and absorbed by your dog's digestive system, so there's a big pile of poop to clean up. One of the first things people notice when feeding their dog a home diet is that the volume of poop goes down and even that it smells better.

Some things to look out for: If the stools are soft but hold their shape, then everything is most likely in good order. If they are too loose to pick up, then your dog may have eaten something that doesn't agree with him or her. Very dark or black stools could mean that he or she has had a bit too much meat; get back to a balanced diet of meat, vegetables and some carbohydrates.

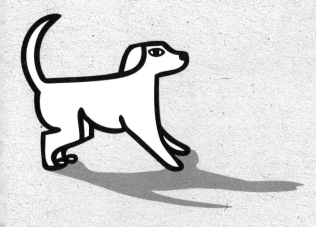

Balanced Breakfasts

Banana Smoothie

Dogs love the taste and texture of bananas—just make sure the banana is ripe. I love using blueberries wherever I can, partly because they are one of Lily's favorite things to eat, but also because they are jam-packed with vitamin C and lots of other antioxidants. This is a great recipe to make for a Sunday breakfast.

· · · · · · · · · · · · · · 🐾 · · · · · · · · · · · · · ·

½ ripe banana, peeled
⅓ cup (50 g) blueberries
½ cup (100 g) plain yogurt
1 tablespoon ground flaxseed

· · · · · · · · · · · · · · 🐾 · · · · · · · · · · · · · ·

Put all the ingredients in a bowl and mash them together.
Serve immediately.

· · · · · · · · · · · · · · 🐾 · · · · · · · · · · · · · ·

Per 4 ounces (100 g):
Calories: 115
Protein: 5%
Fat: 5%

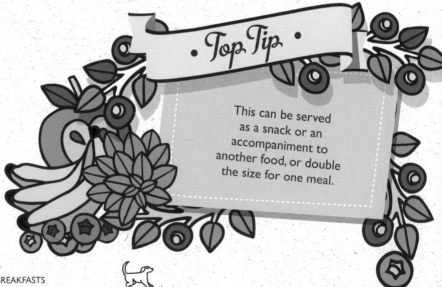

· Top Tip ·

This can be served as a snack or an accompaniment to another food, or double the size for one meal.

Morning Oatmeal

Oats are a wonderful ingredient because they are very digestible and also high in protein. This makes a satisfying and healthy start to the day.

· · · · · · · · · · · · · ✿ · · · · · · · · · · · · ·

1¼ cups (100 g) old-fashioned oats
2½ cups (600 ml) water
1 apple
1 small handful blueberries
1¼ tablespoons ground flaxseed
1 rounded teaspoon dried (or 1¼ tablespoons chopped
fresh) herbs, (see pages 122–23)

· · · · · · · · · · · · · ✿ · · · · · · · · · · · · ·

Put the oats and water in a saucepan and bring to a boil.
Cover and cook for 5 minutes. Leave to cool completely. (This can take about an hour, so you might want to cook the oats the night before, cover and let cool overnight.)

Core and grate the apple and stir it into the cooked oats, along with the blueberries, flaxseed and herbs.

· · · · · · · · · · · · · ✿ · · · · · · · · · · · · ·

Per 4 ounces (100 g):
Calories: 360
Protein: 10%
Fat: 8%

Variations

Stir 1 cup (250 g) cottage cheese into the cooked oats, along with the fruit and herbs.
Add 2 large beaten eggs to the oats before cooking.
Add ½ cup (100 g) cooked, diced chicken or turkey, about 4 ounces.
Mix 6 ounces (200 g) canned salmon into the finished porridge.

Apple and Blueberry Muffins

These are a yummy—and very healthy—treat to share with your dog, but they probably won't be as sweet as you're used to. I've added cottage cheese to this recipe to give the muffins a boost of protein.

Break up the muffins to give them to your dog rather than serving them whole. They'll last longer that way, too! (They should keep fresh for up to 3 days if stored in an airtight container.)

· · · · · · · · · · · · ·❀· · · · · · · · · · · · ·

Makes 20 mini muffins or 10 large ones

1 cup (150 g) brown rice flour (or whole wheat flour)
2 large eggs
½ cup (100 ml) milk
2½ tablespoons olive oil
¼ cup (50 g) cottage cheese
2 small, sweet apples, peeled, cored and grated
⅓ cup (50 g) blueberries
1¼ tablespoons ground flaxseed
1 rounded teaspoon dried herbs or 1¼ tablespoons finely chopped
fresh herbs (see pages 122–23)
1 rounded teaspoon honey (optional)
Vegetable oil for greasing

Preheat the oven to 350°F/180°C. Measure the brown rice flour into a bowl and form a well in the center. Break the eggs into another bowl, pour in the milk and olive oil and beat lightly together. Pour this mixture into the well in the brown rice flour and stir. You should have a nice loose mixture.

Stir in the cottage cheese, grated apple, blueberries, ground flaxseed and herbs. If you want to sweeten the recipe, add the honey. Mix together thoroughly with a spoon.

Lightly grease a muffin or cupcake tin and place a rounded tablespoon of the mixture into each of the cups. Place the tin into the preheated oven and bake for 20 minutes for large muffins, or 10–12 minutes for mini muffins.

Per 4 ounces (100 g):
Calories: 365
Protein: 14%
Fat: 9%

Fruit Salad

It is good to serve your dog fruit as it provides so many health benefits, including lots of vitamin C and antioxidants. It's also a source of soluble fiber—so it's good for digestion, too.

· · · · · · · · · · · · · ·🐾· · · · · · · · · · · · · ·

1 ripe banana
1 apple
⅔ cup (100 g) blueberries

· · · · · · · · · · · · · ·🐾· · · · · · · · · · · · · ·

Peel and chop the banana and peel, core and chop the apple. Mix both together with the blueberries in your dog's bowl.

· · · · · · · · · · · · · ·🐾· · · · · · · · · · · · · ·

Per 4 ounces (100 g):
Calories: 70
Protein: 1%
Fat: 0%

· Top Tip ·

Serve this as a snack rather than as a dessert (i.e., as an additional dish) as fruit could ferment in your dog's stomach and cause gas or indigestion if eaten right after a meaty meal.

Savory Porridge

Lentils and oats make an excellent combination because they are both high protein and low GI, which means they will help your dog feel satisfied for longer, thus—hopefully—eliminating any begging behavior!

Lentils are extremely digestible and so are oats. If this is the very first time you are feeding your dog lentils, then there may be some gas, but once he or she gets used to digesting whole foods, rather than the usual list of animal derivatives present in most pet foods, this should cease to be a problem.

· · · · · · · · · · · · · ✿ · · · · · · · · · · · · ·

1 cup (200 g) lentils
4 cups (900 ml) water
1 cup (75 g) old-fashioned oats
½ cup (100 g) cottage cheese
1 rounded teaspoon finely chopped fresh parsley
1½ cups (about 9 ounces) chopped cooked meat (turkey, chicken, beef or fish)

· · · · · · · · · · · · · ✿ · · · · · · · · · · · · ·

Put the lentils in a pot and cover with the water. Bring to a boil and simmer gently for about 25 minutes or until cooked.

Once the lentils are cooked, add the oats, stir and let cool.

Stir in the cottage cheese (you should have a thick purée), the parsley and the chopped cooked meat.

You can either form the mixture into patties and place them on a plate, or store it in the bowl to use when you need it.

· · · · · · · · · · · · · ✿ · · · · · · · · · · · · ·

Per 4 ounces (100 g):
Calories: 440
Protein: 20%
Fat: 11%

Frittata

Eggs are a really good source of complete protein for dogs. Eggs are better cooked, as raw eggs contain an enzyme that stops the absorption of vitamin B and also carry the risk of salmonella.

This is a recipe you can whip up in no time. If you are very pressed for time, you could just serve the eggs on their own as a scramble.

1 medium russet potato (200 g), peeled and roughly chopped
Water
½ cup (50 g) peas (fresh or frozen)
1 ¼ tablespoons vegetable oil
2 large eggs, beaten

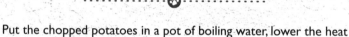

Put the chopped potatoes in a pot of boiling water, lower the heat and simmer until cooked, about 15 minutes. Drain.

Cook the peas in a separate pot of boiling water for a few minutes until heated through. Drain.

Heat the vegetable oil in a frying pan, then pour in the beaten eggs. Place the peas and potatoes on top and cook for 2 minutes. Fold the frittata in half and continue to cook for 2 to 3 minutes more, until the eggs are done.

Remove the pan from the heat and let cool for several minutes until the frittata reaches room temperature. Chop up and serve.

Per 4 ounces (100 g):
Calories: 360
Protein: 21%
Fat: 12%

Healthy Mealtimes

- It may seem that dogs have stomachs of steel, but they can get sick from the same food-borne illnesses that affect people. Here are some things you can do to keep your dog as healthy as possible:

- Always wash your hands before you prepare your dog's food.

- Cook meat thoroughly.

- Prepare and store cooked and raw meat separately from one another and from other foods.

- Once you have thawed a food, do not refreeze it.

- If you put food out for your dog and he or she does not eat it, do not leave it out for longer than two hours; discard it.

- Always keep your dog's food bowl and water bowl clean; wash them after every meal.

Buckwheat Pancakes

Buckwheat is a lovely flour—it has a sweet taste and is also very nutritious. These are easy pancakes to make and you can fill them with all sorts of things to create a nutritious meal. This is also a rather good recipe to share!

1¾ cups (200 g) buckwheat flour
2 cups plus 2 tablespoons (500 ml) milk
2 large eggs, beaten
1 rounded teaspoon vegetable oil

For the filling:
½ cup (100 g) cottage cheese
3⅓ cups (about 4 ounces) fresh spinach leaves, shredded

Measure the flour into a bowl, make a well in the center and pour in the milk and beaten eggs. Whisk the ingredients together, then place the bowl in the fridge for 20 minutes.

Heat the vegetable oil in a frying pan, then pour enough batter into the pan to coat the bottom. Cook for about 30 seconds, then flip the pancake over and cook for a further minute or so.

Put the cottage cheese in the center of the pancake and add the spinach leaves. Roll up the pancake while it's in the pan so the filling heats up. Cut into pieces to serve.

Per 4 ounces (100 g),
without filling:
Calories: 328
Protein: 13%
Fat: 32%

Per 4 ounces (100 g),
including filling:
Calories: 347
Protein: 16%
Fat: 32%

Variations

Replace the spinach leaves and cottage cheese with one of the following:
½ cup (50 g) grated Cheddar cheese
¼ cup (50 g) cream cheese
¼ cup (50 g) lean chopped ham, about 2 ounces

Daily Dinners

Homemade Kibble

This is a great dish as all of the ingredients, except the turkey, are cooked in one pot. You could, of course, just serve this as a stew, but I love the idea of being able to make your own kibble. It takes about an hour, but it's very easy and also very empowering to make a food that has always been a bit of an industry secret.

Turkey is great as it's very low in fat and very digestible, which makes it useful for dogs that are allergic to the usual protein sources—lamb, beef and chicken. Turkey is also handy as it's readily available ground.

This is also a good hypoallergenic recipe that is free of wheat. You'll notice I haven't included peas, which seem always to be part of a dog's menu these days. Peas can be hard to digest for some dogs and therefore can make them gassy.

1 cup and 1 tablespoon (200 g) brown rice
½ cup (100 g) lentils
5 cups (1¼ liters) water
3 medium carrots (200 g), peeled and chopped
1 medium sweet potato (200 g), scrubbed and chopped
1 apple, peeled, cored and chopped, or ½ cup (100 g) unsweetened applesauce
¾ cup (100 g) steel-cut oats
1¼ tablespoons finely chopped fresh parsley
2 small sprigs fresh rosemary, finely chopped
2¼ cups (500 g) ground turkey, about 18 ounces
¼ cup (50 ml) olive, sunflower or canola oil, plus additional oil for greasing

Put the rice and lentils into a saucepan and cover with the water. Bring to a boil, then reduce the heat to medium and cook for 20 minutes.

Once the rice and lentils are cooked, add the chopped carrots, sweet potato and apple to the saucepan. Stir in the oats and chopped herbs and gently simmer for 20 minutes more. Add an extra cup of water if the mixture is too dry. Preheat the oven to 350°F/180°C.

Meanwhile, brown the ground turkey in a separate frying pan. You will need to keep stirring it while it is cooking to prevent it from sticking to the pan as it is very low in fat. It will take about 10 minutes to cook through.

Put half the cooked vegetable and grain mixture into a food processor with half the cooked turkey, add half the oil and pulse until the mixture resembles a thick purée.

Grease 2 cookie sheets and spread the mixture onto one of the sheets so that it is about ¼ inch (5 mm) thick. The mixture will spread slightly so leave a bit of room for this. It is important that the mixture is not too thick because it will prohibit the kibble from cooking through.

Repeat as above using the second cookie sheet and the remaining ingredients.

Place both cookie sheets into the preheated oven and bake for 45 minutes. Turn the kibble over so that it dries through and cook for another 30 to 45 minutes. You should have what looks like two very large cookies. Make sure the kibble is completely cooked through, as any moist bits will get moldy after a couple of days. If it is not fully dried out, leave it in the oven for 20 minutes more.

Reduce the oven temperature to 325°F/160°C. Remove the "kibble cookies" from the oven, cool slightly and cut them into small pieces. Place the pieces back onto the cookie sheets and bake for an additional hour, or until the kibble is completely dried (but not burnt).

Remove the kibble from the oven and let cool completely. It should resemble pieces of broken pita bread. It will keep in the fridge for 10 days.

· · · · · · · · · · · · · · ✾ · · · · · · · · · · · · · ·

Per 4 ounces (100 g):
Calories: 365
Protein: 20%
Fat: 9%

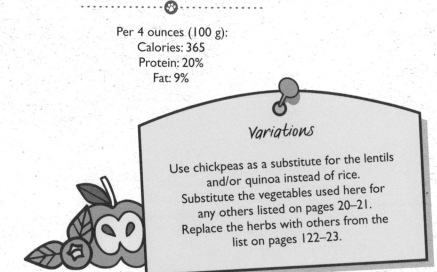

Variations

Use chickpeas as a substitute for the lentils and/or quinoa instead of rice.
Substitute the vegetables used here for any others listed on pages 20–21.
Replace the herbs with others from the list on pages 122–23.

Salmon and Oat Balls

This no-cook recipe offers an easy way to give your dog fish that contains the important omega-3 essential fatty acids. (For an extra omega boost, add a tablespoon of ground flaxseed.) The soft bones in the salmon are also a good source of calcium. The rose hips powder provides a lovely, natural form of vitamin C, while kelp is a rich source of nutrients. This is a good recipe for a sick dog, too.

²⁄₃ cup (100 g) old-fashioned oats
½ cup (100 ml) water
6 ounces (200 g) canned salmon in oil
1 medium carrot, peeled and grated
1 apple, peeled, cored and grated
¼ teaspoon rose hips powder
¼ teaspoon kelp powder
2 tablespoons olive oil

Soak the oats in the water for 15 minutes (this makes them more digestible for your dog).

Empty the can of salmon, including the oil, into a bowl and mash with a fork. (You don't need to remove the pieces of bone—they will dissolve and are a great source of calcium for your dog.)

Add the soaked oats, grated carrot and apple, rose hips powder, kelp powder and oil, and stir together well.

Roll the mixture into small balls in your hands, 1 to 2 tablespoons each. They will keep for 5 days in the fridge or up to 2 months in the freezer.

Per 4 ounces (100 g):
Calories: 200
Protein: 11%
Fat: 9%

Sardine Bake

This recipe is made for dogs that need some time off from meat! Sardines are a fantastic source of omega-3 essential fatty acids and are rich in protein, helping to maintain strong and healthy bones. They are also the best source of vitamin B$_{12}$ of all fish.

· · · · · · · · · · · · ❀ · · · · · · · · · · · · ·

Vegetable oil for greasing
3.75 ounces (120 g) canned sardines in oil
2 medium russet potatoes (400 g), peeled and thinly sliced
½ cup (50 g) peas (fresh or frozen)

· · · · · · · · · · · · ❀ · · · · · · · · · · · · ·

Preheat the oven to 350°F/180°C. Lightly grease an ovenproof dish.

Put the sardines and their oil into a small bowl and mash. Lay half the potato slices in the bottom of the dish, cover with the mashed sardines and peas, then finish with the remainder of the potato slices.

Cover the dish with foil and bake for 30 minutes until cooked through.

Allow to cool to room temperature before serving it to your dog. It will keep, covered, in the fridge for up to 4 days.

· · · · · · · · · · · · ❀ · · · · · · · · · · · · ·

Per 4 ounces (100 g):
Calories: 350
Protein: 23%
Fat: 10%

Super Fish Cakes

Tuna and mackerel have lots of good fats in them in the form of omega-3s and are good for your dog's overall health and shiny coat. Dogs also love the taste of fish and it's great to give them a spectrum of proteins, rather than just relying on chicken and lamb.

· · · · · · · · · · · · · 🐾 · · · · · · · · · · · · ·

3 medium russet potatoes (500 g), peeled and diced
Water
1 cup (50 g) broccoli florets
6 ounces canned tuna in oil
4.375 ounces canned mackerel in oil
1 ¼ tablespoons finely chopped fresh parsley

· · · · · · · · · · · · · 🐾 · · · · · · · · · · · · ·

Put the potatoes in a saucepan and cover with water. Bring to a boil, then reduce the heat and simmer for 20 minutes until cooked. Add the broccoli in with the potatoes for the last 5 minutes of cooking. Drain the vegetables and mash them roughly.

Add the tuna and mackerel, along with their oils, and the parsley and stir together well.

Let cool completely, then form into balls. These will keep, covered, in the fridge for up to 5 days.

· · · · · · · · · · · · · 🐾 · · · · · · · · · · · · ·

Per 4 ounces (100 g):
Calories: 380
Protein: 30%
Fat: 13%

Variations

Replace the potato with butternut squash, peeled, seeded and chopped.
Replace the broccoli with spinach.

• Organic or Not? •

Ideally you would always use organic ingredients when making food for your dog. Unfortunately, the cost of some organic ingredients can be rather high, so as long as you are happy with the food choices you are making, then the ingredients you choose will be fine—and still much better than something cooked up by a mass-produced pet food company
(apart from Lily's Kitchen, of course!).

Here are some key facts about organic ingredients:

• Animals that are reared organically have a better quality of life because they are free to roam outdoors, in their natural habitat.

• No pesticides are used on foods or grass that these animals eat.

• Hormones and antibiotics are not allowed except in exceptional circumstances.

• Organic production usually has a much lower yield since animals and pastures have not been pumped up with steroids, fertilizers and other artificial additives.

• Organic farming is better for the environment in general—fewer pesticides and artificial fertilizers means more wildlife and a better overall ecosystem.

• Organic certification is a guarantee that no genetically modified ingredients have been used and no artificial ingredients have been used that have not been previously approved by the certifier.

Wonderful One-Pot

This is a satisfying recipe that contains a wide range of nutrients. There's a rainbow of fruits and vegetables here, too, together with the ideal combination of lentils, rice and oats. Spoon out however much you need for your dog's meal.

Broccoli is a super vegetable for dogs that is full of nutrition as well as a cancer-fighting ingredient, but Lily tends to leave behind a neat pile of it in her bowl unless I chop it up very finely!

½ cup (100 g) brown rice
½ cup (100 g) lentils
4¼ cups cold water
1¼ (50 g) old-fashioned oats
2½ tablespoons olive oil
3 to 4 boneless chicken thighs, diced (about 1¼ cups/300 g/11 ounces)
3 medium carrots (200 g), peeled and finely diced
2 cups (100 g) broccoli florets
14.75 ounces (400 g) canned salmon
1 medium apple (200 g), peeled, cored and grated
⅓ cup (50 g) blueberries
1¼ tablespoons ground flaxseed

Rinse the brown rice and lentils under cold running water. It is best to soak them overnight first, because they're more digestible that way, but don't worry if you don't have time.

Put the rice and lentils into a saucepan and add the cold water. Bring to a boil, reduce the heat, cover and simmer for 30 minutes until the rice and lentils are cooked. Stir in the oats and let sit for 5 minutes.

Heat 1½ teaspoons of the olive oil in a frying pan, add the diced chicken and cook for 10 minutes.

Meanwhile, put the diced carrots into a pot of simmering water and cook for 5 minutes, then add the broccoli and cook for 5 minutes more. Drain.

Open the can of salmon and flake gently. Don't worry about the bones as they are soft and a very good source of calcium for your dog.

Put the grated apples, blueberries and flaxseed into a large bowl and stir in all the other ingredients. This will keep in the fridge for up to 4 days.

Per 4 ounces (100 g):
Calories: 400
Protein: 25%
Fat: 18%

Top Tip

Never feed your dog raw salmon, which can contain parasites that are particularly harmful to dogs.

Chicken and Rice Balls

If you have a dog that seems to prefer bland food, this is a good recipe to make. It provides a balance of vegetables, carbohydrates and protein. If your dog is overweight or has an intolerance to fat, discard the skin of the chicken after it has been cooked. This is a good recipe for a sick dog, too.

· · · · · · · · · · · · ·⊗· · · · · · · · · · · · ·

4 or 5 chicken thighs
Water
3 medium carrots (200 g), chopped
3 medium parsnips (200 g), chopped
½ cup (100 g) white rice
1 rounded teaspoon finely chopped fresh parsley or rosemary
⅓ cup (50 g) old-fashioned oats

· · · · · · · · · · · · ·⊗· · · · · · · · · · · · ·

Put the chicken thighs in a saucepan and cover with water. Bring to a boil, reduce the heat and simmer for 20 to 30 minutes.

Put the chopped carrots and parsnips into another saucepan, cover with water and bring to a boil. Reduce the heat and simmer until soft, about 10 to 15 minutes. Drain, then return the vegetables to the pot and mash together.

Once the chicken is cooked, place on a plate, remove the bones from the thighs and chop the meat and skin into small pieces.

Put the rice in the saucepan with the stock, bring to a boil, reduce the heat, cover and simmer until cooked. (Follow the package instructions as cooking times vary depending on the type of rice used.)

Put the chicken pieces into a bowl with the cooked rice, mashed vegetables and dried herbs and mix together well.

Spread the oats on a large plate. Form the chicken, rice and vegetable mixture into small balls—about 2 to 3 tablespoons each, depending on the size of your dog—and roll them in the oats to coat.

The finished chicken and rice balls can be stored in the fridge for up to 5 days or you can freeze them for 2 months.

· · · · · · · · · · · · · ❁ · · · · · · · · · · · · ·

Per 4 ounces (100 g):
Calories: 400
Protein: 20%
Fat: 18%

· Top Tip ·

The stock will be full of nutrients, so keep it in the fridge for up to a week to use for another recipe, such as Morning Oatmeal (page 35) or Calming Oats (page 105).

Rice with Meat

This is a good easy recipe and one that is a favorite in our household. As with most of the recipes in this book, it's gluten-free.

½ teaspoon sunflower oil
2 cups (450 g) ground beef, about 16 ounces
1¼ cups (200 g) brown rice
3 cups (85 g) fresh spinach
2 medium carrots, grated
1 rounded teaspoon finely chopped fresh parsley
2½ cups (600 ml) water
¼ cup (50 ml) plain yogurt (optional)

Heat the sunflower oil in a frying pan and brown the ground beef, breaking it up with a wooden spoon.

Add the rice, spinach, grated carrots, parsley and water. Stir, then cover and cook on a gentle simmer until the rice absorbs the water—this usually takes about 30 minutes.

Remove the lid and let cool. Store in the fridge for up to 5 days.

Before serving, you can stir in the yogurt for some extra probiotic goodness, if you wish.

Per 4 ounces (100 g):
Calories: 400
Protein: 22%
Fat: 17%

Variations

Replace the ground beef with ground turkey, lamb, chicken or pork.

Sunshine Stew

This is a lovely, colorful and satisfying stew. I've used lamb, but you could also use ground turkey, beef or chicken. I've added some liver, too, for extra nutrition and taste.

· · · · · · · · · · · · · · 🐾 · · · · · · · · · · · · · ·

1 cup (200 g) lentils (green or red)
½ cup (100 g) pearl barley
4¼ cups (1 liter) water
1 butternut squash (700 g), peeled, seeded and diced
4 ounces (100 g) green beans, trimmed and chopped (about 30 beans)
1¾ cups (400 g) ground lamb, about 14 ounces
4 or 5 chicken livers (200 g), cut into small pieces
1¼ tablespoons salmon oil or flaxseed oil
1 rounded teaspoon dried (or 1¼ tablespoons chopped
fresh) herbs (see pages 122–23)

· · · · · · · · · · · · · · 🐾 · · · · · · · · · · · · · ·

Rinse the lentils and pearl barley and put them in a saucepan with the water. Bring to a boil, reduce the heat and simmer for 30 minutes. Drain.

Meanwhile, put the butternut squash and green beans into another pot and cover with water. Bring to a boil, reduce the heat and simmer gently for 20 minutes.

Heat a frying pan over medium heat. Add the ground lamb and liver pieces and fry gently for 15 minutes until cooked through.

Combine all the cooked ingredients and stir in the salmon
or flaxseed oil. Add the herbs.

You can either serve this as a stew or process it lightly in a food processor (if your dog tends to leave the veggies and just go for the meat). If you process it, you can roll the mixture into balls and keep them in the fridge for 5 days or in the freezer for 2 months and just pull out the amount you need for a meal.

· · · · · · · · · · · · · · 🐾 · · · · · · · · · · · · · ·

Per 4 ounces (100 g):
Calories: 330
Protein: 32%
Fat: 7%

Lamb, Lentil and Vegetable Stew

This is a wholesome stew that is satisfying to make for your dog on a rainy afternoon. It contains an exceptional variety of fruits and vegetables and is low in fat. If your dog loves broccoli, add an additional cup.

········· ·········

1 cup (100 g) brown rice and/or lentils
3 cups (700 ml) cold water
18 ounces (500 g) lamb (leg or shoulder), diced
1 chicken or turkey liver (50 g), cut into small pieces
½ butternut squash (350 g), peeled and diced
½ cup (50 g) peas (fresh or frozen)
1 cup (100 g) broccoli florets
2 sweet apples, peeled, cored and diced
1⅓ cups (50 g) fresh spinach, shredded
⅓ cup (50 g) blueberries
1¼ tablespoons ground flaxseed
1 rounded teaspoon dried (or 1¼ tablespoons finely chopped fresh) herbs (see pages 122–23)

Rinse the brown rice and/or lentils in cold water. Add them to a large saucepan with the water. Bring to a boil, reduce the heat and simmer for 10 minutes.

Add the diced lamb and liver pieces to the saucepan (making sure there is enough water to cover) and cook for 10 minutes.

Add the diced squash to the saucepan and cook for 15 minutes. Add the peas, broccoli, diced apples and shredded spinach leaves and cook 15 minutes more.

Finally, add the blueberries and cook for 5 minutes more.

Remove the saucepan from the heat and stir in the ground flaxseed and herbs. Leave to cool to room temperature before serving. Any remaining stew can be refrigerated for up to 3 days.

Per 4 ounces (100 g):
Calories: 500
Protein: 26%
Fat: 11%

Top Tip

If you want to include some extra fat because your dog needs building up then add 1¼ tablespoons of flaxseed oil and 1¼ tablespoons of salmon oil to each meal.

Meat Loaf

This recipe looks and smells delicious. It's also handy because it will keep for a week in the fridge, so you can just slice it up and use it as you need it.

Vegetable oil for greasing
4 to 5 chicken or turkey livers (200 g)
Water
2 cups ground beef (450 g), about 16 ounces
2 medium russet potatoes (400 g), peeled and grated
1 large carrot (150 g), peeled and grated
2 large eggs
⅔ cup (50 g) old-fashioned oats
1¼ tablespoons finely chopped fresh parsley and/or rosemary

Preheat the oven to 350°F/180°C. Grease a loaf pan well. Cook the livers in simmering water for 3 minutes, then drain and chop finely.

Put the ground beef in a bowl and stir in the grated potatoes and carrot and the chopped liver.

In a separate bowl, lightly beat the eggs, then add them to the mixture along with the oats and herbs. Mix together with a spoon or clean hands.

Scoop the mixture into the greased loaf pan and lightly flatten the top. Bake in the preheated oven for 1 to 1½ hours.

Remove the meat loaf from the oven and let stand for 20 minutes or so to make it easier to slice.

The meat loaf will keep for a week in the fridge or up to 2 months in the freezer.

Per 4 ounces (100 g):
Calories: 430
Protein: 31%
Fat: 20%

• Top Tip •

You can also make individual
portions using greased muffin
tins. Reduce the baking time to
50 minutes.

Traditional Gravy

This is a traditional gravy, but with no salt added and very low in fat. You can serve this alongside kibble, even storebought if you like. The kelp powder provides a wide range of nutrients and minerals such as iodine.

18 ounces (500 g) beef bones from your butcher
8½ cups (2 liters) water
2 medium carrots, peeled and chopped
2 russet potatoes, peeled and chopped
½ teaspoon kelp powder

Put the bones in a large saucepan and add the water. Cover the pan, bring to a boil, reduce the heat and simmer gently for an hour.

Put the chopped carrots and potatoes into another saucepan and cover with water. Bring to a boil, reduce the heat and simmer until soft. Drain, then mash or purée the vegetables.

Take the bones off the heat and pour the mixture into a strainer over a clean saucepan. Discard everything that is left in the strainer. Add the stock to the mashed vegetables, then add the kelp powder and stir well to combine.

The gravy can be kept in the fridge for a week or you can freeze it in an ice cube tray for up to 2 months and use as needed.

Per 4 ounces (100 g):
Calories: 60
Protein: 8%
Fat: 1%

Superfood Gravy

Most gravies that people enjoy are not good for dogs because they are far too salty. Here, instead, is a gravy that is perfect for dogs—meaty, rich, delicious and with some antioxidants, so it's healthy as well. Organ meat in the form of liver gives it a vitamin E boost, too.

Once prepared, you can pour the gravy into an ice cube tray, freeze it and use the cubes whenever you need them. The frozen gravy cubes will keep for up to two months. Warm the gravy to room temperature before feeding it to your dog. You can serve it alongside any kibble.

· · · · · · · · · · · · · · 🐾 · · · · · · · · · · · · · ·

1¼ tablespoons vegetable oil
2¼ cups (500 g) ground turkey, about 18 ounces
2 to 3 chicken or turkey livers (100 g)
½ cup (50 g) frozen peas
3 cups (700 ml) water

· · · · · · · · · · · · · · 🐾 · · · · · · · · · · · · · ·

Heat the vegetable oil in a frying pan and brown the ground turkey and livers.

Once the meat is browned, add the peas, then pour in the water. Put a lid on the pan and simmer for 30 minutes.

Remove the pan from the heat and let the mixture cool slightly, then place it in a food processor or blender and process until smooth. It may remain a bit grainy once you have done this, but your dog won't mind!

· · · · · · · · · · · · · · 🐾 · · · · · · · · · · · · · ·

Per 4 ounces (100 g):
Calories: 330
Protein: 19%
Fat: 6%

· Special Meals ·

· for Special Days ·

Celebration Cupcakes

Our family famously invited my daughter's entire class over for a picnic at the local park to celebrate Lily's first birthday (to the horror of the school's new headmistress, who was appalled to think she had joined the kind of school where even dogs' birthdays were celebrated). I served these cupcakes to Lily and her dog friends, who devoured them all! They look very appetizing and are also very healthy.

· · · · · · · · · · · · · · 🐾 · · · · · · · · · · · · · ·

Makes 6

Vegetable oil for greasing
1 cup (150 g) brown rice flour
2 large eggs
½ cup (100 ml) milk
2½ tablespoons olive oil
½ cup (50 g) grated Cheddar cheese
1¼ tablespoons ground flaxseed
1¼ tablespoons finely chopped fresh parsley
¼ cup (50 g) cream cheese

Preheat the oven to 350°F/180°C. Lightly grease a muffin or cupcake tin.

Measure the brown rice flour into a clean bowl and make a well in the center.

Break the eggs into another bowl and pour in the milk and olive oil. Beat the ingredients lightly together. Add this mixture to the brown rice flour and stir well. You should have a nice loose mixture. Add the grated Cheddar cheese, ground flaxseed and parsley and mix together with a spoon.

Spoon about 2 tablespoons of the mixture into each cup of the tin. Transfer the tin to the preheated oven and bake for 15 minutes until the cupcake tops are a light golden color.

Remove the cupcakes from the oven and place on a wire rack to cool. Once they are completely cool, spread a generous teaspoon of the cream cheese on top of each cupcake.

Per 4 ounces (100 g):
Calories: 445
Protein: 16%
Fat: 20%

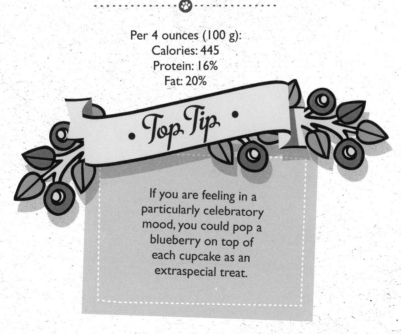

Top Tip

If you are feeling in a particularly celebratory mood, you could pop a blueberry on top of each cupcake as an extraspecial treat.

Birthday Cake

My family loves celebrating Lily's birthday by baking her something extra special. This cake is easy to slice up and share with any other doggy friends that are invited over for lunch. You can also easily decorate it so that the cake looks appealing and appetizing . . . though Lily, of course, doesn't really care what it looks like as long as it tastes delicious!

Vegetable oil for greasing
1¼ cups and 2 tablespoons (300 g) ground lamb, about 11 ounces
1⅓ cups (150 g) unbleached all-purpose flour
⅔ cup (50 g) old-fashioned oats
⅓ cup (50 g) ground sunflower seeds
½ cup (100 g) cottage cheese
⅔ cup (150 ml) water
2 large eggs, beaten

To decorate:
½ cup and 1 tablespoon (150 g) low-fat cream cheese
4 slices (100 g) Cheddar cheese, cut into small squares
1¼ tablespoons finely chopped parsley

• • • • • • • • • • • • ✿ • • • • • • • • • • • • •

Preheat the oven to 350°F/180°C. Lightly grease an 8-inch (20 cm) cake pan.

Place the ground lamb, flour, oats, ground sunflower seeds, cottage cheese, water and eggs into a bowl and mix together well. The mixture will have a meat loaf–like consistency.

Transfer the mixture into the prepared cake pan and bake the cake for about 45 minutes, or until cooked through. Remove the pan from the oven, let stand for a few minutes and remove the cake from the pan. Place the cake on a wire rack to cool completely.

"Ice" the top of the cooled cake with low-fat cream cheese. Use the Cheddar cheese squares to decorate the top of the cake and sprinkle with the chopped parsley.

• • • • • • • • • • • • ✿ • • • • • • • • • • • • •

Per 4 ounces (100 g):
Calories: 520
Protein: 23%
Fat: 27%

Holiday Feast

The holidays always include a feast of food that is quite rich and heavy. You will want to share the holiday cheer with your pet, but try to avoid feeding him tidbits that are high in fat, such as cheese, sausages and ham. Ideally, keep the treats to mealtimes so that your beautifully trained dog doesn't turn into a scavenging wide-eyed beggar! Here's a holiday dinner he can happily and healthily share with you.

· · · · · · · · · · · · · ·🐾· · · · · · · · · · · · · ·

2 cups (250 g) chopped cooked turkey, about 8 ounces
1 cooked mild sausage, chopped (see Tip)
½ cup (100 g) mashed potatoes
6 cooked Brussels sprouts (100 g), chopped

· · · · · · · · · · · · · ·🐾· · · · · · · · · · · · · ·

Put the turkey and chopped sausage into a bowl. Add the mashed potatoes and Brussels sprouts and mash together.

· · · · · · · · · · · · · ·🐾· · · · · · · · · · · · · ·

Per 4 ounces (100 g):
Calories: 460
Protein: 33%
Fat: 25%

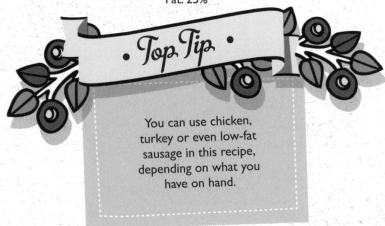

· Top Tip ·

You can use chicken, turkey or even low-fat sausage in this recipe, depending on what you have on hand.

Lamb Cupcakes

These are ideal meaty treats for special occasions when you know a few dogs will be visiting. It's easier not to use paper liners so you don't have to pull them off before serving.

· · · · · · · · · · · · 🐾 · · · · · · · · · · · ·

Makes 12

Vegetable oil for greasing
2¼ cups (500 g) ground lamb, about 18 ounces
1¼ cups (200 g) brown rice flour
⅔ cup (50 g) old-fashioned oats
1 large egg, beaten

· · · · · · · · · · · · 🐾 · · · · · · · · · · · ·

Preheat the oven to 350°F/180°C. Lightly grease a muffin or cupcake tin.

Put all the ingredients into a bowl and mix together well.

Spoon a heaping tablespoon of the mixture into each cup of the tin, then bake for 30 minutes, or until cooked through.

Let cool completely before serving. These cupcakes will keep for 5 days in the fridge.

· · · · · · · · · · · · 🐾 · · · · · · · · · · · ·

Per 4 ounces (100 g):
Calories: 620
Protein: 30%
Fat: 13%

Top Tip

If you are making these for a special event, why not try "icing" them with low-fat cream cheese and using alfalfa seeds as sprinkles?

Meat Pies

Meat pies are a traditional festive favorite in some parts of the world. Here is a recipe that dogs will love, so that they, too, have their own meat pies to eat during the holidays.

I often add ginger to this recipe as it's good for the joints and helpful, too, as a blood cleanser.

Thanks to the pie pastry, these pies are rather fattening, so even though it is the festive season, serve only one or two a day. If your dog has two, reduce his or her regular amount of food accordingly.

· · · · · · · · · · · · · ·❀· · · · · · · · · · · · · ·

Makes 8

Vegetable oil for greasing
2 cups (450 g) ground turkey, about 16 ounces
1 ¼ tablespoons finely chopped fresh parsley
¼ rounded teaspoon ground ginger (optional)

For the pastry:
1 ¾ cups (200 g) unbleached all-purpose flour
⅓ cup and 4 teaspoons (100 ml) oil
1 large egg, beaten
½ cup (50 g) Cheddar or other hard cheese
Water

Preheat the oven to 350°F/180°C. Lightly grease a cupcake or muffin tin.

Put the ground turkey into a bowl and stir in the chopped parsley and ground ginger (if using). Set aside.

To make the pastry, measure 1¾ cups of flour into a bowl and add the oil, beaten egg and grated cheese. Stir together with a spoon.

Put the dough onto a lightly floured surface and roll out. Cut the dough into 16 discs using a cookie or pastry cutter and use half of them to line 8 cups of the prepared tin.

Add 2 tablespoons of the turkey mixture into each cup. Brush the edges of the remaining pastry discs with water and use them to top each of the pies, pressing them gently around the edges to seal. Pierce the top of each pie with a fork to allow steam to escape while cooking.

Place the pan in the oven and bake for 30 minutes. Once cooked, remove the pies from the oven and transfer to a wire rack to cool.

You can store the meat pies in the fridge for up to a week.

Per 4 ounces (100 g):
Calories: 620
Protein: 28%
Fat: 13%

Top Tip

If your dog is gluten intolerant, replace the wheat flour with spelt flour or a 100 percent gluten-free flour and add 2 teaspoons (10 ml) additional oil. The spelt dough is easy to handle but can be a little crumbly when cooked.

Halloween Hotpot

When Halloween comes along, winter is just around the corner.
Lily's coat begins to look rather bushy at this time of the year—she
resembles a small woolly lamb—and there's also a lot more huddling
up around the fireplace or in front of the oven. It seems only right to
make her something warming to eat.

· · · · · · · · · · · · · ·🐾· · · · · · · · · · · · ·

3½ cups (400 g) cubed and peeled fresh pumpkin, about 14 ounces
¼ cup (50 g) brown rice
1 cup (250 ml) boiling water
1 tablespoon vegetable oil
1⅓ cup (300 g) minced lamb, about 11 ounces
1 rounded teaspoon dried (or 1¼ tablespoons finely chopped fresh)
herbs (see pages 122–23)

· · · · · · · · · · · · · ·🐾· · · · · · · · · · · · ·

Preheat the oven to 350°F/180°C.

Place the pumpkin cubes in a roasting pan and bake for 20 to 25 minutes.

Meanwhile, put the rice into a saucepan, cover with the boiling water and simmer, covered, until cooked. (Follow the package instructions as cooking time will vary depending on the type of rice used.)

Heat the oil in a frying pan. Add the minced lamb and gently fry for 15 minutes, then stir in the herbs. Add the cooked rice and pumpkin to the pan and stir together.

Let cool before serving a portion to your dog. The remainder will keep in the fridge for up to 4 days.

. . . . ❀ . . . .

Per 4 ounces (100 g):
Calories: 640
Protein: 30%
Fat: 12%

Top Tip

Baking the pumpkin rather than boiling it lets it retain more of its nutrients.

Tuna and Sardine Fish Balls

Tuna is really good for the joints and internal organs, especially the heart, and it also gives dogs a lovely coat. Sardines are also very high in omega-3s, vitamin D and selenium. I have added ground flaxseed to this recipe for an extra omega-3 boost.

························🐾························

4.5 ounces (130 g) canned tuna in sunflower oil
3.75 ounces (100 g) canned sardines in oil
1 medium russet potato (200 g)
3⅔ cups (100 g) fresh spinach, or ¼ cup (50 g) frozen spinach
1¼ tablespoons ground flaxseed
1¼ tablespoons chopped fresh parsley

························🐾························

Open the cans of tuna and sardines and pour the entire contents into a large bowl. Check for and discard any large, hard sardine bones. Mash the fish together and set aside.

Peel and roughly chop the potato, add to a pot of boiling water and cook for 15 minutes. Add the spinach for the last 5 minutes of cooking time.

Drain the potato and spinach and mash them using a potato masher or fork. Add the mashed vegetables, ground flaxseed and chopped parsley and mix together.

Once the mixture is cool enough to handle, form it into about 6 balls, using your hands or 2 wooden spoons, and place the balls on a plate. (Two of these balls will be enough for a meal for a small to medium dog.)

··············· ✻ ···············

Per 4 ounces (100 g):
Calories: 340
Protein: 33%
Fat: 20%

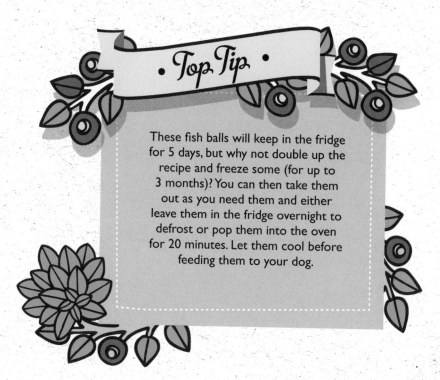

· *Top Tip* ·

These fish balls will keep in the fridge for 5 days, but why not double up the recipe and freeze some (for up to 3 months)? You can then take them out as you need them and either leave them in the fridge overnight to defrost or pop them into the oven for 20 minutes. Let them cool before feeding them to your dog.

Tasty Treats

Tasty Treats

Giving dogs a treat is a lovely way of acknowledging them for something good they have done. These treats are all delicious, easy to make and as different from the store-bought ready-made "treats" as you can imagine. Unfortunately, most of the mass-produced treats—and this includes the so-called "natural" ones—are far from the description on the pack.

The worst culprits are those described as "semimoist." These have very strong preservatives added to stop them from becoming moldy. To give you an idea, here are some of the ingredients that go into semimoist treats: phosphoric acid, artificial antioxidants such as propyl gallate (a carcinogenic in rat studies), citric acid and a mold inhibitor—potassium sorbate. Not natural at all!

The other things to watch out for in store-bought treats are the levels of fat and sugar. Dogs adore both but will pile on the pounds if you are feeding them lots of high-fat treats, and sugary ones are obviously not great for their teeth, either.

The best treats or snacks you can give your dog are those made in your own kitchen—and that way you know exactly what's gone into the recipe, too! These treats are suitable for puppies, for whom you'll need treats at the ready for training, and for older dogs, who will appreciate a tasty tidbit of something delicious during the day.

Spelt and Sunflower Treats

These are good chunky treats to take with you on walks. They won't crumble in your pocket and they contain lots of healthy oils. If your dog is wheat-intolerant, spelt flour may be a good alternative; although it is a form of wheat, it is a variety that dogs are less likely to have a problem with.

Vegetable oil for greasing
¼ cup and 2 tablespoons (50 g) raw, unsalted sunflower seeds
1⅔ cups (200 g) spelt flour
1¼ tablespoons ground flaxseed
6¼ tablespoons olive oil
½ teaspoon finely chopped fresh parsley
½ teaspoon finely chopped fresh rosemary
⅔ cup (150 ml) water or milk

Preheat the oven to 350°F/180°C. Lightly grease a cookie sheet.

Roughly chop the sunflower seeds using either a knife or a mortar and pestle. Put the seeds into a bowl with all the other ingredients and mix everything together.

Take a small amount of the dough, roll it into a ball the size of a golf ball and place it onto the prepared cookie sheet. When your cookie sheet is full of small balls, press your thumb into the middle of each one to flatten slightly. Bake for 30 minutes until cooked through.

Transfer the treats from the oven onto a cooling rack and allow to cool. They will keep in a sealed container for up to a week.

Per 4 ounces (100 g):
Calories: 560
Protein: 11%
Fat: 30%

Oatmeal Cookies

I love cookie recipes that have no wheat flour. Oats are low GI and a very good source of soluble protein and fiber for your dog. Oat flour is made from ground oats and is a popular gluten-free option. This is one of the recipes that Lily has to fight me for! These cookies are a very healthy treat and a particularly good way to give your dog some added fiber. They are ideal as a midmorning snack.

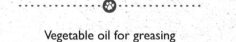

Vegetable oil for greasing
2¼ cups (250 g) oat flour
1¼ tablespoons oil or fat, such as chicken fat or beef drippings
¼ cup (50 ml) boiling water (optional)

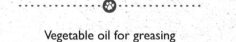

Preheat the oven to 350°F/180°C. Lightly grease a cookie sheet.

Place the oat flour in a bowl and make a well in the center to pour the liquid into.

Put the oil into the well, or if you are using a hard fat, such as chicken, spoon it into the bowl and pour the boiling water over the fat to melt it. Stir with a knife or spoon and it will quickly form a dough.

Lightly dust a clean work surface with some of the remaining oat flour and turn the dough out onto it. You can either roll out the dough to around ½-inch (1 cm) thickness or just flatten it into shape with your hands.

Cut the dough into small pieces or use a small cookie cutter to cut it into discs. Place the discs on the cookie sheet and bake for about 20 minutes.

These cookies will keep for up to 2 weeks in an airtight container.

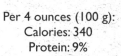

Per 4 ounces (100 g):
Calories: 340
Protein: 9%
Fat: 14%

Variations

Mix one of the following into the oat flour
before adding the oil or fat:
1¼ tablespoons chopped fresh parsley
1¼ tablespoons grated Cheddar or other
hard cheese
1 rounded teaspoon blackstrap molasses
1 rounded teaspoon finely chopped dried apple

Peanut Butter and Buckwheat Kisses

Despite having the word *wheat* in it, buckwheat flour is in fact gluten-free and has a sweet, nutty taste. Peanut butter is a palatable fat to add if you have a finicky dog and want an alternative to animal fat. It also has a substantial level of protein.

Vegetable oil for greasing
1¾ cups (200 g) buckwheat flour, plus extra for dusting
½ cup and 1 tablespoon (50 g) steel-cut oats
1 heaping teaspoon blackstrap molasses
½ cup (100 ml) boiling water
⅓ cup (100 g) unsweetened creamy peanut butter

Preheat the oven to 350°F/180°C. Lightly grease a cookie sheet.

Put the buckwheat flour and oats into a bowl.

Measure the blackstrap molasses into a small bowl. Pour the boiling water over the molasses and stir until dissolved. Add the peanut butter and stir. Add to the bowl with the flour and oats and mix together to form a soft dough. (If it is a little dry, add a few tablespoons of water.)

Lightly flour a clean work surface with additional buckwheat flour and turn out the dough onto it. Roll small pieces of the dough into balls about half the size of a golf ball. Put them on the prepared cookie sheet and press down gently on each ball with your thumb. Bake for 25 minutes.

Let the kisses cool (they should be quite hard), then store them in a sealed container. They should keep for at least a week.

Per 4 ounces (100 g):
Calories: 400
Protein: 13%
Fat: 30%

Cheesy Oat Bars

These are a great addition to your pet's pantry. They are handy to take on a long journey if there hasn't been time for breakfast (or supper) and you know you aren't going to be home to scoop out some food for your dog. They are also good as a big treat if you're on a long walk and dinner seems like a long way off.

This recipe makes about eight bars. Lily, who weighs 26 pounds (12 kg), will have two of them as an emergency meal replacement or one as a big treat.

. . . . 🐾 . . . .

Vegetable oil for greasing
2½ cups (200 g) old-fashioned oats
2½ tablespoons honey
½ cup (50 g) grated Cheddar cheese
¼ cup (50 ml) sunflower oil
¼ cup and 2 tablespoons finely chopped fresh parsley or rosemary
1 large egg, beaten

. . . . 🐾 . . . .

Preheat the oven to 350°F/180°C. Lightly grease an 8-inch (20 cm) baking pan.

Put all of the ingredients into a saucepan. Cook over low heat for a couple of minutes, stirring so the cheese doesn't stick to the bottom of the pan. Pour the mixture into the baking pan.

Smooth down the mixture firmly using the back of a wooden spoon. Bake for 20 minutes, or until golden brown.

Remove from the oven and let cool slightly before cutting into 8 equal bars. Let cool completely in the pan. The bars will keep in an airtight container for 10 days in the fridge.

. . . . 🐾 . . . .

Per 4 ounces (100 g):
Calories: 420
Protein: 10%
Fat: 16%

Cheesy Puffs

These are fun to make and you can keep them for ten days in a sealed jar. They have a small amount of cheese in them, which dogs love, as well as some flaxseed for an omega-3 boost. However, because they are high in fat, you should limit your dog to two a day.

Vegetable oil for greasing
Unbleached, all-purpose flour for dusting
1 sheet (200 g) puff pastry, about 7 ounces, thawed
½ cup (50 g) grated Cheddar cheese
¼ cup and 2 tablespoons (50 g) ground flaxseed

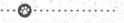

Preheat the oven to 350°F/180°C. Lightly grease
a cookie sheet.

On a lightly floured work surface, roll out the puff pastry into a rough square shape. Scatter the grated cheese over the surface, then sprinkle with the ground flaxseed. Use your hand to press these toppings into the pastry.

Cut the pastry into long strips, then cut the strips into 1¼-inch (3 cm) pieces. (If you prefer, you can cut the pastry into disc shapes with a small cookie cutter instead.)

Place the strips on the cookie sheet and bake for 20 minutes.

Let them cool completely, then store them in an airtight container.

Per 4 ounces (100 g):
Calories: 500
Protein: 12%
Fat: 30%

Fishy Treats

Some dogs go crazy for fish. These treats are a good way of getting them to eat a really healthy snack that they will adore. They are also very easy to make. You can feed your dog up to two or three a day.

· · · · · · · · · · · · 🐾 · · · · · · · · · · · · ·

Vegetable oil for greasing
7 ounces (200 g) canned tuna in oil or canned salmon in oil
1 large egg, beaten
¾ cup and 2 tablespoons (100 g) unbleached all-purpose flour

· · · · · · · · · · · · 🐾 · · · · · · · · · · · · ·

Preheat the oven to 350°F/180°C. Lightly grease a cookie sheet.

Empty the fish and its oil into a bowl and flake with a fork. Add the beaten egg and stir well to combine.

Add the flour and mix together by hand so that you have a lumpy dough. You can either roll out the dough and cut it into small squares or pick up small pieces of dough and roll them into little balls.

Place the shapes on the cookie sheet and bake for 20 minutes, or until golden brown and cooked through.

Once they are cool, you can store them in a container in the fridge for up to 2 weeks.

· · · · · · · · · · · · 🐾 · · · · · · · · · · · · ·

Per 4 ounces (100 g):
Calories: 380
Protein: 38%
Fat: 13%

Mini Meaty Balls

These delicious training treats smell very appetizing. If you have a dog who tends to disappear in the park the moment you get there, make sure you show him or her that you have a couple of these handy so your dog will come racing back to you! Don't feed your dog too many at a time, though, because they are very high in calories.

· · · · · · · · · · · · · · 🐾 · · · · · · · · · · · · · ·

1⅓ cups (300 g) ground lamb or turkey, about 11 ounces
1 large egg
¼ cup and 1 tablespoon (50 g) brown rice flour
1 sprig parsley, stems removed
Vegetable oil for greasing

· · · · · · · · · · · · · 🐾 · · · · · · · · · · · · ·

Put all of the ingredients except the oil into a food processor and blend until they form a soft consistency like bread dough.

Lightly grease a cookie sheet. Roll the mixture into marble-size balls and place them on the cookie sheet. Refrigerate for about an hour so they hold their shape when they are cooked. Meanwhile, preheat the oven to 350°F/180°C.

Bake the meaty balls for 45 minutes. They should be hard rather than crumbly. If you have used lamb, then drain off the fat.

· · · · · · · · · · · · · 🐾 · · · · · · · · · · · · ·

Per 4 ounces (100 g):
Calories: 780
Protein: 42%
Fat: 18%

· Table Scraps ·

You might not think twice about feeding your dog the leftovers after a meal. But you do need to make sure that you are not sharing scraps that are salty or peppery. Giving a dog some gravy seems like a nice idea, but bear in mind that the gravy will have been seasoned for humans, so it's likely to be far too salty. Why not cook up some homemade Traditional Gravy (page 62) or Superfood Gravy (page 63) instead?

The other thing to avoid is feeding your dog table scraps that are too fatty, like the skin of a chicken you've cooked for the family. Doing so could cause a bout of pancreatitis, if your dog is sensitive to fat. If you want to give your dog something special to eat, the tasty treats in this chapter are designed just for him.

Fresh produce

Power Treats

These small liver cake treats are designed for dogs who turn their nose up at baked biscuit treats. I defy a dog to refuse these! They are bursting with really great ingredients, each of which has a specific nutritional purpose. This recipe has a two-stage cooking process to make sure the treats are properly cooked through.

Vegetable oil for greasing
2 large eggs
½ pound (250 g) fresh beef liver, roughly chopped
½ cup (50 g) grated Cheddar cheese
½ heaping teaspoon blackstrap molasses
2½ cups and 2 tablespoons (300 g) buckwheat or spelt flour

Preheat the oven to 350°F/180°C. Lightly grease a cookie sheet.

Break the eggs into the bowl of a food processor and add the liver, grated cheese and blackstrap molasses. Pulse to purée together.

Add in the flour and pulse to combine. You should now have a soft dough. The dough will be quite sticky so it's a good idea to put plenty of flour on your hands to handle it.

Take out the dough and put it straight onto the prepared cookie sheet. Flatten it down with your hands so that it is about ½ inch (1 cm) thick. Alternatively, roll the dough into a cylinder on a lightly floured surface and slice it into discs. Bake for about 20 minutes.

Remove the cookie sheet from the oven and cut the dough into small squares; tiny size if you have a small dog and larger if your dog is bigger—you know what size treat your dog is used to!

Reduce the oven temperature to 300°F/150°C. Put the treats back into the oven and let dry completely for 2 hours.

Remove the treats from the oven and let them cool completely before storing in an airtight container. They keep well in the fridge for up to 2 weeks.

⚙

Per 4 ounces (100 g):
Calories: 390
Protein: 30%
Fat: 14%

• Top Tip •

I like to add the eggs whole as there's lots of good nutrition in the shells: some natural calcium, as well as glucosamine, which is good for joints. Crush up the shells with your hands or a mortar and pestle so that the shell pieces are as small as possible, and add them to the food processor with the other ingredients.

Pure Liver Treats

There are moments when you need a piece of something very tasty to coax your dog away from a rabbit (or a fox, in Lily's case). These treats are very easy to prepare and you can make them plain and simple or sprinkle them with a teaspoon of dried alfalfa or parsley before you put them into the oven.

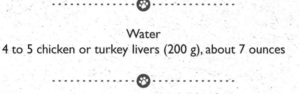

Water
4 to 5 chicken or turkey livers (200 g), about 7 ounces

Preheat the oven to 350°F/180°C. Line a cookie sheet with parchment paper.

Pop the livers into a saucepan of boiling water for 5 minutes. This makes them much easier to slice. (You can just chop them without boiling them, but they are rather slithery.)

Once they are roughly chopped, place them onto the prepared cookie sheet and bake for 45 minutes to 1 hour. You need the livers to be thoroughly dry so they will keep well.

Once the liver treats are ready, remove them from the oven and let them cool on the cookie sheet. You can keep them in an airtight container in the fridge for 2 weeks or freeze them for up to 2 months.

Per 4 ounces (100 g):
Calories: 425
Protein: 60%
Fat: 20%

Dried Apple Rings

This is another simple treat that is very healthy for your dog and virtually fat free! Lily loves apples of all varieties, and this is a good low-fat treat you can serve without worrying about putting weight on your dog. Dogs love anything sweet, so these treats make a nice change from the usual savory treats.

⸺⸺⸺⸺ ❀ ⸺⸺⸺⸺

4 to 5 apples—any variety but make sure they are not bruised

⸺⸺⸺⸺ ❀ ⸺⸺⸺⸺

Preheat the oven to 325°F/160°C.

Peel and core the apples and slice into ¼-inch (6 mm) rings. Place the rings on a nonstick cookie sheet and put them into the oven to bake for about 6 hours.

They should be dry and leathery when they are done, rather than crispy (although crispy is also fine). The more moisture you take out of them, the longer they will keep. They will keep for 2 to 4 weeks in an airtight container depending on how dry they are.

⸺⸺⸺⸺ ❀ ⸺⸺⸺⸺

Per 4 ounces (100 g):
Calories: 58
Protein: 1%
Fat: 0%

• Top Tip •

You can also make this recipe using pears, whole strawberries and bananas sliced lengthwise. Just make sure they do not burn.

Fruity Granola Squares

Dogs love fruit and one of Lily's favorites is apples, which is why I like to include them in a lot of recipes. Apples are a good source of vitamin C and fiber, and they also provide sweetness, which dogs like. Blackstrap molasses is a great source of B vitamins and iron.

Vegetable oil for greasing
¼ cup and 2 tablespoons (50 g) sunflower seeds
2 cups (200 g) old-fashioned oats
½ cup (100 g) unsweetened applesauce (see Tip)
¼ cup sunflower oil
1¼ tablespoons blackstrap molasses
1¼ tablespoons rose hips powder

Preheat the oven to 350°F/180°C. Lightly grease an 8-inch (20 cm) square pan.

Grind the sunflower seeds in a food processor, or crush them using a mortar and pestle, until they are roughly ground. (This is so your dog can make good use of the nutrition—if they are whole they will simply pass straight through and not be digested properly).

Add the crushed sunflower seeds and oats to a saucepan and stir to combine.

Combine the applesauce, sunflower oil, blackstrap molasses and rose hips powder in a bowl and stir to combine.

Pour this mixture over the dry ingredients in the pan. Stir gently over medium heat until the molasses has dissolved, then transfer to the pan. Smooth down the mixture firmly using the back of a wooden spoon. Bake for 20 minutes, or until golden brown.

Remove the fruity granola from the oven and allow it to cool slightly, then cut it up into squares or rectangles. Let cool completely in the pan. The squares will keep for a week in a sealed container.

· · · · · · · · · · · · · ✿ · · · · · · · · · · · · ·

Per 4 ounces (100 g):
Calories: 420
Protein: 8%
Fat: 17%

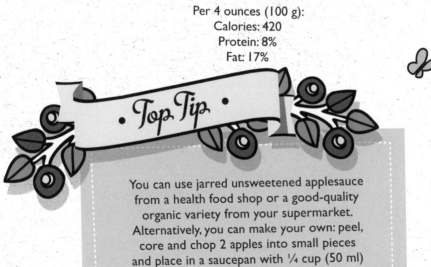

Top Tip

You can use jarred unsweetened applesauce from a health food shop or a good-quality organic variety from your supermarket. Alternatively, you can make your own: peel, core and chop 2 apples into small pieces and place in a saucepan with ¼ cup (50 ml) water to prevent sticking. Simmer over low heat for 10 minutes.

Treats for a Hot Day

There are lots of healthy treats you can make for your dog that will help him or her cool down when it's a sweltering day. Here are some simple ideas for frozen treats. Follow the instructions and once frozen, transfer the treats to a plastic bag and return to the freezer to use as and when required.

· · · · · · · · · · · · · · · ❁ · · · · · · · · · · · · · · ·

Peanut Butter Pops

Put ¼ cup (65 g) of unsweetened creamy peanut butter into a bowl and stir in 1¾ cups (400 ml) of water to loosen the consistency. Pour the mixture into an ice cube tray and freeze.

Per 4 ounces (100 g):
Calories: 140
Protein: 11%
Fat: 18%

· · · · · · · · · · · · · · · ❁ · · · · · · · · · · · · · · ·

Apple Pops

In a large measuring cup, mix ¾ cup (175 ml) of unsweetened apple juice and ¾ cup (175 ml) of water. Pour the mixture into an ice cube tray and freeze.

Per 4 ounces (100 g):
Calories: 30
Protein: 2%
Fat: 0%

· · · · · · · · · · · · ✿ · · · · · · · · · · · ·

Frozen Fruity Treats

As a variation on the above Apple Pops recipe, pop blueberries, chopped strawberries and/or raspberries into each section and freeze.

Per 4 ounces (100 g):
Calories: 30
Protein: 2%
Fat: 0%

· · · · · · · · · · · · ✿ · · · · · · · · · · · ·

Frozen Banana Treats

Peel and slice a ripe banana. Put the slices on a plate or baking sheet and put into the freezer.

Per 4 ounces (100 g):
Calories: 95
Protein: 1%
Fat: 0%

Top Tip

These treats are quite slurpy. Dogs like to lick them and push them around, so it's best to give them the treats outside or on a hard floor.

Recovery Recipes

Recovery Recipes

We get to know our dogs so well that we can tell the minute something is off. When Lily isn't feeling well, she loses her terrier-like independence and follows me everywhere. It's at times like these I wish she could talk and tell me exactly what she is feeling and where it hurts.

If your dog loses his or her appetite, it's always a good idea to visit the vet to see what's going on, in case it's something serious. It could, for example, be some sort of food intolerance or allergy.

If you suspect your dog may have an allergy, see if you can make the link between what they've been eating and any reaction this may have caused. Probably one of the most problematic meats for dogs is chicken, as

derivatives of it are so widely used in dog foods. If you suspect this might be the case, you could try serving fish, turkey or beef instead.

Dogs love sweet things, so when your dog is not feeling too well and needs coaxing to eat something, it's great to include a variety of sweet vegetables and fruit to help restore his appetite.

The recovery recipes are not designed to be used on a long-term basis, but just for two to four days. If you have fallen into feeding your dog "chicken and rice" to help through a bout of illness, be sure to go back to complete recipes once your dog is better. Dogs who are fed chicken meat with (with no organ meat added) rice for too long, for example, can develop extremely serious illnesses.

Pick-Me-Up Breakfast

If your dog needs a nutritious breakfast that will bring his or her energy up, then this is a quick and easy choice. There are no exotic ingredients in this recipe, but the ingredients here all provide a healthy and tasty pick-me-up for when your dog is feeling a bit low—perhaps after an operation. Eggs are an excellent source of protein and can be fed to your dog once or twice a week.

········•·········

½ cup (50 g) old-fashioned oats
½ cup (100 ml) water or milk
1¼ tablespoons vegetable oil
2 large eggs, beaten
½ cup (100 g) cottage cheese
1 rounded teaspoon dried (or 1¼ tablespoons finely chopped fresh) herbs (see pages 122–23)

········•·········

Soak the oats in the water or milk for 15 minutes.

Heat the oil in a frying pan, then add the beaten egg and scramble it. Once cooked, stir in the cottage cheese, soaked oats and herbs.

Allow to cool to room temperature before serving.

········•·········

Per 4 ounces (100 g):
Calories: 320
Protein: 28%
Fat: 15%

Chicken and Barley Soup

The classic combination of chicken and pearl barley is the essence of a comforting homemade meal. When I last made this, Lily and I shared the recipe! This soup also looks very pretty, with its lovely creamy orange color.

Orange vegetables are great for dogs and according to a 2005 issue of the *Journal of the American Veterinary Medical Association*, dogs that consume orange or yellow vegetables at least three times a week are at a lower risk of developing cancer. It must be because these vegetables have a high level of beta-carotene, which will also help give your dog a beautiful coat.

· · · · · · · · · · · · 🐾 · · · · · · · · · · · ·

Chicken carcass from a roast
6⅓ cups (1½ liters) water
3 medium carrots (200 g), about 7 ounces
2 apples
3 medium sweet potatoes (500 g), about 18 ounces
½ cup (100 g) pearl barley, rinsed under cold water
1 rounded teaspoon ground flaxseed

· · · · · · · · · · · · · · 🐾 · · · · · · · · · · · ·

Put the chicken carcass into a large pot and cover with the water. Bring to a boil, then lower the heat and simmer, covered, for about an hour.

Meanwhile, prepare the vegetables: peel and roughly chop the carrots and apples, making sure you remove the apple seeds. Peel or scrub the sweet potatoes and chop roughly.

Remove the chicken pot from the heat and pour the contents into a large strainer or colander over a bowl. You will now have a delicious-smelling stock in the bowl and the leftover carcass in the strainer.

When the carcass is cool enough for you to handle, pick off any bits of chicken that are left and set them aside.

Put the strained liquid into a clean pot and add the pearl barley and prepared vegetables. Cover with the lid, bring to a boil, and then lower the heat and simmer gently for about an hour.

Let cool, add in any pieces of chicken from the carcass and purée the mixture in a food processor until smooth. It may be more like a purée than a soup, but that's fine and your dog will love it!

You can keep this soup in the fridge for up to 5 days or freeze it for up to 2 months. Serve with the ground flaxseed sprinkled on top.

· · · · · · · · · · · · · ⊗ · · · · · · · · · · · · · ·

Per 4 ounces (100 g):
Calories: 220
Protein: 28%
Fat: 1%

Top Tip

You could also add some homemade kibble pieces to this soup as "croutons" (see pages 46–47).

Soothing Meals for Upset Tummies

If your dog has a bout of diarrhea, you will need to serve something very bland that will settle him or her again. Diarrhea can have all sorts of causes, but the most likely one is that your dog has eaten something he or she shouldn't have while out on a walk or in the garden. If your dog's stomach does not settle after a day or two, or if he or she is vomiting, you should contact your vet for advice. Here are a few ideas for suitable foods for dogs suffering from diarrhea:

· · · · · · · · · · · · · ❁ · · · · · · · · · · · · ·

Chicken Pasta

1 cup (100 g) dried pasta
4 cups (1 liter) low-sodium chicken stock

Cook the pasta in the chicken stock according to the package directions. Drain, cool to room temperature and then serve a small amount to your dog. You can keep any unused pasta in the fridge for up to 2 days.

Per 4 ounces (100 g):
Calories: 490
Protein: 11%
Fat: 2%

· Top Tip ·

If your dog is better the next day you can cook up some ground meat—something low in fat like chicken or turkey—and mix this with the remaining pasta.

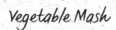

Vegetable Mash

1 medium russet potato (200 g), peeled and diced
3 medium carrots (200 g), peeled and diced

Add the diced vegetables to a pot of boiling water and cook for 15 minutes. Drain the vegetables, then mash together. Allow to cool to room temperature before serving a small amount to your dog.

Per 4 ounces (100 g):
Calories: 290
Protein: 7%
Fat: 0%

Calming Oats

Oats are said to build and strengthen, and they are ideal if you have a dog that needs a calming, soothing meal.

1½ cups (100 g) old-fashioned oats
2½ cups water

Put the oats into a pot with the water and cook over medium-high heat for 10 minutes. Leave to cool completely in the pot. A bit of patience is needed here as it will take an hour or so for the mixture to cool enough for your dog to eat it safely.

Per 4 ounces (100 g):
Calories: 380
Protein: 9%
Fat: 5%

Stew for Sad Dogs

On days when your dog seems under the weather and in need of some TLC, this warming, heartening stew with its lovely selection of sweet vegetables and fruit will help get his or her tail wagging again.

18 ounces fresh turkey (breast or thighs) or 2¼ cups ground turkey (500 g)
1¼ tablespoons vegetable oil
3 or 4 parsnips, peeled and diced
6 large carrots, peeled or scrubbed and diced
2¼ cups (200 g) old-fashioned oats
1¼ cups water
2 medium Gala or Macintosh apples
2½ tablespoons honey
1 rounded teaspoon dried (or 1¼ tablespoons finely chopped fresh) herbs (see pages 122–23)
1 rounded teaspoon ground flaxseed

Dice or chop the turkey meat, making sure there are no bones, or if you are using ground turkey, just crumble it slightly. Heat the oil in a large pot, add the meat and brown over a medium heat.

Add the diced parsnips and carrots, oats and water, which should be enough to cover all the ingredients. Bring to a boil, then reduce the heat, cover and simmer for about 20 minutes.

Once the stew has cooked, peel, core and grate the apples and stir into the stew along with the remaining ingredients.

Feed the stew to your dog once it is cool enough to eat. If it's a cold day, you can serve it warm, but not hot. It will keep in the fridge for 4 days.

Per 4 ounces (100 g):
Calories: 350
Protein: 19%
Fat: 8%

Quick Doggy Ice Cream

Lily adores the taste of yogurt! Yogurt is, of course, full of bacteria that are good for your dog's stomach and will help him or her digest food well. This is a good recipe to make if your dog is on a course of antibiotics.

· · · · · · · · · · · · · · ·🐾· · · · · · · · · · · · · ·

⅔ cup (150 ml) plain yogurt
½ cup (50 g) blueberries

· · · · · · · · · · · · · · ·🐾· · · · · · · · · · · · · ·

In a small bowl, stir together the yogurt and blueberries. You can either keep the blueberries whole or mash them in with the yogurt.

Spoon equal portions into an ice cube tray and freeze. Once frozen you can pop a couple of cubes out for your dog.

· · · · · · · · · · · · · · ·🐾· · · · · · · · · · · · · ·

Per 4 ounces (100 g):
Calories: 60
Protein: 4%
Fat: 1%

· Top Tip ·

You can make this recipe using any of the fruits described on pages 22–23.

Comforting Meals · for Old Hounds

Old Hounds

I don't think there's a fixed age when dogs become "old hounds." However, you will probably notice your dog getting a bit slower and more prone to hanging around in bed for longer periods. Old dogs are also likely to get a bit stiffer in their joints and may become more cantankerous and lose interest in performing their usual tricks.

When it becomes clear that your dog has reached his or her dotage (usually from about eight years old onwards, depending on breed and level of activity), you will probably need to reduce the amount of food by about 20 percent. Older dogs don't run around as much as younger ones, so they need fewer calories if they are to avoid piling on the pounds.

It's important to make sure your older dog has good mental stimulation and gets at least 20 minutes of exercise every day. You can definitely teach an old dog new tricks and it's a great way to keep him or her happy and stimulated!

You'll also need to keep an eye out for any joint issues or possible hereditary health issues. There is a range of holistic remedies with which you can treat your dog if he or she does develop joint problems, and there are plenty of holistic and homeopathic vets who will be able to help you choose the right treatment.

All of the recipes in this book are suitable for older dogs, but the ones in this chapter are especially good as they have lots of extra nutritional benefits and are particularly delicious, to tempt older dogs that may have lost their appetite.

Salmon Bake

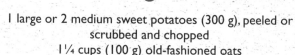

Salmon is a fantastic fish, rich in nutrients. It contains lots of omega-3s, which are good for overall health and will benefit your dog's coat, skin, joints and internal organs. Salmon also aids brain development, and some studies have shown that it can ward off arthritis.

· · · · · · · · · · · · · ✦ · · · · · · · · · · · · ·

1 large or 2 medium sweet potatoes (300 g), peeled or
scrubbed and chopped
1¼ cups (100 g) old-fashioned oats
Water
7 ounces (200 g) canned salmon in oil
3 or 4 medium carrots (200 g), peeled and grated
2 apples, peeled, cored and grated
½ cup (100 g) plain yogurt
1 large egg, beaten
1¼ tablespoons ground flaxseed

· · · · · · · · · · · · · ✦ · · · · · · · · · · · · ·

Preheat the oven to 350°F/180°C. Put the chopped sweet potatoes into a pot with water to cover. Bring to a boil, reduce the heat and simmer for 15 minutes until cooked, then drain and mash roughly.

Meanwhile, put the oats in a pot with water
and cook for 10 minutes.

Add the salmon and oil to a large bowl and mash. Add the mashed sweet potatoes, cooked oats, grated carrot and apple, yogurt and beaten egg. Mix together well. Spoon the mixture into an ovenproof dish and bake for 40 minutes.

Remove the bake from the oven and sprinkle the top with the ground flaxseed. Allow it to cool before serving. It will keep up to 4 days in the fridge.

· · · · · · · · · · · · · ✦ · · · · · · · · · · · · ·

Per 4 ounces (100 g):
Calories: 350
Protein: 18%
Fat: 9%

Comforting Chicken Stew

Older dogs tend to have a lower metabolism and need less food than they did when younger. They often become more picky about what they eat, so feeding them something delicious as well as nutritious is crucial. I firmly believe that you can help make sure your dog has a long and healthy life by providing a really good diet. It's important to keep the immune system as strong as possible by feeding your dog plenty of vegetables, fruits and good-quality proteins. And keep him or her away from preservative-laden "treats" and "chews!"

· · · · · · · · · · · · ·❀· · · · · · · · · · · · ·

1 medium russet potato (200 g), peeled and chopped into small pieces
2 medium carrots (100 g), peeled and chopped into small pieces
2 cups (100 g) broccoli florets
4 to 5 chicken thighs (500 g), about 18 ounces
2 to 3 chicken or turkey livers, about 4 ounces (100 g)
⅓ cup (50 g) blueberries
1¼ teaspoons flaxseed oil
¾ teaspoon rose hips powder
¾ teaspoon ground flaxseed

Put the potato and carrots into a pot of water, bring to a boil, then reduce the heat, cover and simmer for 15 minutes. Add the broccoli to the saucepan for the last 5 minutes of cooking time.

Put the chicken and liver in a pot with water to cover. Bring to a boil, then reduce the heat, cover and simmer gently for 15 to 20 minutes until the chicken is cooked.

Drain the chicken and livers, cool and then chop into small pieces, removing and discarding any chicken bones. Place in a large mixing bowl.

Drain the vegetables and add to the chopped meat along with the blueberries, flaxseed oil, rose hips powder and ground flaxseed. Stir well to combine.

Spoon out enough for your dog's meal, then cover the remainder and store in the fridge for up to 4 days.

Per 4 ounces (100 g):
Calories: 450
Protein: 32%
Fat: 30%

Wholesome Hash

Turmeric is good for older dogs, as it helps with the joints and circulation and is also anti-inflammatory. It's also important to include plenty of good oils in your dog's diet at this stage to help with lubricating the joints and promoting, shiny coat and overall health.

· · · · · · · · · · · · · · ✿ · · · · · · · · · · · · · · ·

¾ cup (150 g) brown rice
3 cups (700 ml) water
⅔ cup (50 g) old-fashioned oats
1¾ cups (400 g) ground beef
3½ cups (200 g) green leafy vegetable, such as spinach
or cabbage, shredded
1 medium apple (100 g)
½ cup (50 g) ground flaxseed
1¼ tablespoons salmon oil
1 rounded teaspoon dried (or 1¼ tablespoons finely chopped fresh)
herbs (see pages 122–23)
1 rounded teaspoon turmeric

· · · · · · · · · · · · · · ✿ · · · · · · · · · · · · · ·

Put the rice into a strainer and rinse under running water, then add to a saucepan with the water. Bring to a boil, then reduce the heat, cover and simmer for 30 minutes, or until cooked. Stir in the oats and leave for 5 minutes.

Meanwhile, over medium heat, brown the ground beef in a frying pan until cooked through, about 15 minutes. Cook the greens in a little water until softened.

Peel, core and grate the apple. Place in a large bowl with the cooked rice and oats, ground beef, greens and remaining ingredients and mix thoroughly.

Serve a portion to your dog and store the remainder, covered, in the fridge for up to 4 days.

· · · · · · · · · · · · · · ✿ · · · · · · · · · · · · · ·

Per 4 ounces (100 g):
Calories: 580
Protein: 24%
Fat: 20%

· Digestibility of Food ·

The digestibility of the food you feed your pet is really important. If the food is properly digested, your pet will make really good use of all the nutrition available in the ingredients and just poop out what he or she doesn't need. If you feed your dog good food, there's less waste!

When nutrients are properly absorbed in the small intestine, the remainder of the bowel is allowed to rest and fewer undigested nutrients go on to the large intestine.

If your dog has a particularly hard time digesting food and it seems that everything you serve goes straight through him or her, then do try some of the wholesome recipes in this book. Choose the ones that have a single source of protein, e.g., just lamb or chicken or turkey, together with a gluten-free carbohydrate like rice, lentils or potato.

Dogs just love real food made from fresh ingredients

Winter Hotpot

This is a warming meal that will give your old hound a healthy, nutritious boost. I've chosen some winter favorites here—oats and pearl barley, which are both low GI and will therefore help your dog feel fuller for longer, together with some seasonal vegetables. The vegetables provide a rainbow of colors to maximize nutrition and help boost immunity. The herbs used here—rose hips powder and parsley—all have healing properties and are full of antioxidants for optimum health.

· · · · · · · · · · · · · 🐾 · · · · · · · · · · · · ·

¾ cup (150 g) pearl barley
3 cups (700 ml) water
2 or 3 medium russet potatoes (500 g), peeled and roughly chopped
2 medium carrots (100 g), peeled and roughly chopped
15 green beans (50 g), trimmed and finely chopped
1 cup (100 g) broccoli florets, finely chopped
2¼ cups (500 g) ground lamb, turkey or beef, about 18 ounces
1¼ tablespoons vegetable oil (optional, see instructions)
1¼ cups (100 g) old-fashioned oats
3¼ teaspoon rose hips powder
1 rounded teaspoon chopped fresh parsley

· · · · · · · · · · · · · 🐾 · · · · · · · · · · · · ·

Put the pearl barley in a pot with the water. Bring to a boil, then reduce the heat, cover and simmer for about 40 minutes, until the pearl barley is soft.

Put the chopped potatoes, carrots and green beans into a large pot with water to cover. Bring to a boil, then reduce the heat and simmer for about 20 minutes until all the vegetables are soft. Add the broccoli to the pot for the last 5 minutes of cooking time.

Meanwhile, add the ground meat to a frying pan and brown over medium to high heat for about 10 minutes, breaking it up regularly, until it is thoroughly cooked. If you are using turkey, which is a very lean meat, add a tablespoon of oil to the pan before cooking to prevent sticking.

Once the vegetables are cooked, remove the pan from the heat and stir in the oats. Let sit for 5 minutes, then add the cooked meat, cooked pearl barley, rose hips powder and chopped parsley. Stir the whole mixture, breaking up any lumpy vegetables and then let cool.

This will keep in the fridge for 4 days.

· · · · · · · · · · · · · ⊗ · · · · · · · · · · · · ·

Per 4 ounces (100 g):
Calories: 500
Protein: 20%
Fat: 12%

· Top Tip ·

I recommend chopping the green beans as finely as you can; otherwise, if your dog is anything like Lily, they will be neatly left in the bowl at the end of the meal. If I chop them up into small pieces, Lily doesn't notice them and will eat them up with everything else.

Supergrain Medley

This is a great recipe to which to add meat, for example the leftovers from a Sunday roast, and some vegetables to make a balanced meal. These supergrains should make up around 30 percent of the dish.

· · · · · · · · · · · · · ❀ · · · · · · · · · · · · ·

½ cup (100 g) brown rice
½ cup (100 g) quinoa
½ cup (100 g) pearled barley
4¼ cups (1 liter) water

· · · · · · · · · · · · · ❀ · · · · · · · · · · · · ·

Put all the grains into a strainer and rinse under cold running water. If you have time, soak them overnight (doing so will help retain more of their nutrition and they will also cook more quickly).

Put the grains into a saucepan with the water. Bring to a boil, then reduce the heat, cover and simmer for 30 minutes, or until they are soft.

Remove the cover and let cool before feeding it to your dog. Store, covered, in the fridge for up to a week.

· · · · · · · · · · · · · ❀ · · · · · · · · · · · · ·

Per 4 ounces (100 g):
Calories: 360
Protein: 10%
Fat: 4%

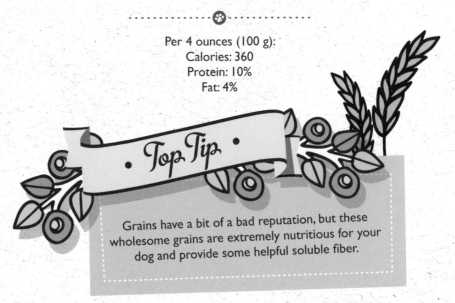

Top Tip

Grains have a bit of a bad reputation, but these wholesome grains are extremely nutritious for your dog and provide some helpful soluble fiber.

Carrot Cakes

These treats are bursting with carroty goodness. Lily loves carrots and it's good for her to occasionally have a nonmeaty treat that's also very satisfying. These carrot cakes have a comforting taste and aroma, and if you are feeding them to your older dog, they will also supply a little energy burst thanks to their natural sweetness.

· · · · · · · · · · · · · ❁ · · · · · · · · · · · · ·

Vegetable oil for greasing
2 large carrots (150 g), peeled and grated
⅔ cup (50 g) old-fashioned oats
½ cup (100 ml) milk
⅔ cup (100 g) brown rice flour
1 rounded teaspoon molasses
½ cup (100 g) unsweetened applesauce
1¼ teaspoons vegetable oil
⅓ cup (50 g) blueberries (optional)

· · · · · · · · · · · · · ❁ · · · · · · · · · · · · ·

Preheat the oven to 350°F/180°C. Lightly grease a cookie sheet.

Put all of the ingredients into a mixing bowl and combine thoroughly.

Drop 2-tablespoon-size balls of the mixture onto the prepared cookie sheet and bake for 30 minutes.

These cakes will keep for up to a week in a sealed container.

· · · · · · · · · · · · · ❁ · · · · · · · · · · · · ·

Per 4 ounces (100 g):
Calories: 350
Protein: 7%
Fat: 10%

One of the best things about cooking for your dog is that you can tailor the meals to provide what your dog needs at the time and add in some healthy extras, such as certain herbs and spices. (Herbs are the leaves of the plant and spices are made from the roots, flowers, seeds, bark or berries of the plant.)

Dogs have evolved to eat herbs in nature over the centuries and indeed I often hear of dogs chewing on rosemary bushes or eating mint from the garden. There's something naturally nutritious about including herbs in your dog's food.

It's worth remembering that our most commonly used medicines have their origins in the herbs and plants of the natural world.

I like to use certain herbs regularly. You're unlikely to grow many of them in your garden, but if you search online you will find several companies that can supply them to you. Ideally, use organic or wildcrafted herbs, which are grown native to their habitat, have had as little interference as possible and have not been exposed to pollutants, pesticides or artificial fertilizers. If you are able to use fresh herbs—for example mint, parsley, rosemary or thyme—so much the better. As a general guideline, I teaspoon of dried is the equivalent of 1 tablespoon of finely chopped fresh herbs. (If you're using ground herbs, you can safely use the same quantity as specified for dried.)

All the herbs listed here are safe to use at home in moderation. You can buy them in dried or powder form and then mix them together to make your own combination anytime a recipe calls for herbs, based on your dog's preferences and needs.

If your dog has a specific medical condition that needs treating, then you should consult a vet who specializes in herbal treatments so that you can be sure your dog is getting the right dosage to help the specific condition that needs treating. If your dog is pregnant, you will need to check whether the herbs you want to use are suitable.

Here is a list of some of my favorite herbs that are safe to use for your dog. You can put a tablespoon of each in a jar, mix them together, and keep the jar in your cupboard. Then add the required amount of your "superherb" mixture to recipes. Try to use dried herbs that are less than six months old so they still have their potency.

Alfalfa

A bit of a wonder herb as it contains a good variety of nutrients such as vitamin K, alfalfa is useful for when your dog is feeling under the weather. It is also very high in protein. It is often recommended for dogs with joint pain or arthritis and it is reputed to have anticancer properties and to help with mental agility, so it is particularly good for older dogs. It is also known as a good treatment for bad breath.

Burdock root

A herb with lots of medicinal attributes, burdock root is used as a general tonic and is helpful in treating skin problems thanks to its antifungal properties. It is considered to be a blood cleanser and purifier and a tonic for the liver and kidneys.

Celery seeds

Good as a detoxifier and helpful therefore for treating bladder and urinary infections as well as arthritis, celery seeds are also known to have a calming effect on the digestive system and can be helpful to relieve gas.

Chickweed

A soothing herb to help with digestion and stomach upsets, chickweed is also a traditional remedy for arthritis.

Cleavers

A traditional cleanser of the liver and detoxifier of the lymphatic system, cleavers is a rich source of vitamin C and helps soothe skin complaints.

Dandelion

A very gentle herb with many supportive and restorative benefits, dandelion is packed with many essential vitamins and minerals. The leaves are used as a diuretic and are good for the liver and digestive system, and the root, too, can be used as a digestive and liver tonic.

Kelp powder

Rich in essential minerals such as iodine, kelp is a favorite with show dogs as it's known to help with maintaining a glossy, shiny coat and strong healthy teeth.

Marigold petals

This is a good cleansing herb for the organs and skin.

Milk thistle

The seeds from this herb are full of antioxidants and are widely used to detoxify the liver and help keep it healthy.

Mint

A beneficial herb for digestion and bloating, mint also helps to freshen breath.

Nettles

A particularly rich source of minerals and vitamins (especially iron), nettles are a good blood purifier and are helpful with skin conditions and allergies. You can also pick your own young nettles (wearing gloves, of course!), cover them with water and simmer for 10 minutes. When cool, add a few tablespoons of the liquid and cooked leaves to your dog's food as a good overall tonic.

Parsley

Parsley is a must-have in your herbal pharmacy: Both leaves and stems are very nutritious and contain lots of vitamins, minerals and fiber. Try to use fresh parsley if you can. (Note: This does not include spring parsley, which can be toxic.)

Rose hips powder

One of my favorite herbs, rose hips are one of nature's richest natural sources of vitamin C, which helps strengthen the immune system to keep your dog really healthy.

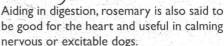

Rosemary

Aiding in digestion, rosemary is also said to be good for the heart and useful in calming nervous or excitable dogs.

Thyme

Thyme can be used to help treat kennel cough and its antiseptic qualities are good if your dog has sore gums. (Note: This does not include Spanish thyme, which can be toxic.)

Turmeric

This spice has anti-inflammatory properties and helps with blood cleansing. It is often given to dogs (and humans) to treat arthritis.

The Lily's Kitchen Story

My dog, Lily, was allergic to all the pet foods I bought for her; she broke out in rashes and then developed itchy ears and skin. Her fur also never seemed to look healthy. I became obsessed with trying to get to the bottom of why her skin was in such bad condition. My brother, who is a vet, thought it could be related to her food.

So I started cooking for Lily, making her fresh meals every day to see if this would make a difference. Within a couple of weeks, her skin and ears had calmed down, and after another two weeks all her "hot spots" had disappeared. She stopped looking like a faded old broom and her fur became healthy and shiny. She also lost that rather pungent "doggy smell," which many owners put up with and eventually become immune to.

Although delighted with the results, however, I was horrified that the food I had been feeding her had been causing these problems. I couldn't believe how blindly I had chosen food for her, believing all the claims on the package label. I felt sure there must be other people like me; indeed, my brother told me

that of the numerous pet owners coming into his office with their dogs and cats, many had pets with dietary issues.

I decided that something needed to be done about the problem. I wasn't especially keen on cooking for Lily every day; I really wanted something ready-made that I could trust 100 percent to be good for her. After all, she shows me such devotion, and I felt that I had let her down by choosing the wrong food for her.

The next step was spending eighteen months talking to a wide range of vets, both conventional and homeopathic, as well as nutritionists and pet food experts. With their help, I began to put together a list of perfect ingredients for pets, and we started Lily's Kitchen with three recipes. It then took another year to find commercial kitchens who wanted to work with us—most of them turned us down the moment they saw the kinds of ingredients we wanted to make our food with. After visiting more than thirty kitchens, I found the ones that were perfect for us.

We launched the Lily's Kitchen line in November 2008 and almost immediately gained a loyal following. Like me, many pet owners had struggled to find something really healthy to feed their pets. People could see this was real food—not "chunk and jelly" that smelled revolting or dry food they had to open at arms' length because of the overwhelming stench of rancid grease.

We are now a team of eleven people and we all feel very proud of what we do. It's a privilege to be in a position to make such a difference to animals' quality of life.

My days are really varied, but my favorite part of my job is developing new products in our kitchen. I've always had an interest in nutrition and healthy eating, and I'm always on the hunt for new ingredients.

While I'm creating a new recipe, I tend to home in on an exciting new ingredient that has a medicinal benefit and build my recipe around this. For example, we have just launched some wonderful new treats called "Power Flowers." I really loved the idea of using turmeric for dogs because this spice has a long list of healing properties and is said to be very good for joints. So I put this together with some other ingredients, such as blackstrap molasses, which is full of B vitamins and very good for the blood.

I love the fact that we've created recipes that are really healthy for cats and dogs and that are filled with really good things so our pets can enjoy healthy meals and healthy lives.

For more on the Lily's Kitchen line, visit lilyskitchen.com.

Index

Acknowledgments

I'd like to acknowledge all the lovely people at Lily's Kitchen I'm lucky enough to work with. They have been very supportive while I have been "under cover" writing this book!

I'd like to thank our in-house vet, Holly Mash, who is an inspirational vet always looking for a holistic alternative to the conventional route to wellness for pets. She has been invaluable with all her knowledge of herbs and nutrition.

I'd also like to thank Jeanette Quainton, who is our specialist nutritionist and has helped me with the nutritional information for the book. She is endlessly patient when I ask for advice on all sorts of ingredients that are not usually used in standard pet foods and has helped make our formulations satisfying and nutritious.

Thanks to the team at Ebury Press who have been so excited and enthusiastic about publishing this book. Many thanks to Sarah Such, Sara Pearson and Anne McDowall, and to Petra Borner for creating the original illustration for the Lily's Kitchen foods. And thanks to Mad River for their tireless enthusiasm in designing this book.

Thanks also to The Experiment for allowing this book to reach its North American audience, including my American editor Cara Bedick, assistant managing editor Molly Cavanaugh, publisher Matthew Lore, and everyone else who pitched in on this edition. The book also wouldn't have been possible without the recipe conversion and testing skills of Linda Zimmerman.

Thank you to my family and friends, especially my brother Bob the Vet—it seems like only yesterday that I met up with you after your interview at the Royal Veterinary School! Thank you to my friends for their endless encouragement and enthusiasm.

I'd especially like to acknowledge my partner, Kim, for all her support and for creating the peace and space in order for me to write this book. And I'd like to thank my daughter, Holly, for always being enthusiastic and for the endless cups of tea she provided for me while I was busy writing.

Last but not least, a big thank you to Lily. Without her I wouldn't truly understand the meaning of unconditional love. Thank you, too, Lily, for always being a keen taster of all my recipes!

636.7083 Morrison, Henrietta.
MOR
        Dinner for dogs.

$15.95

DATE		
SEP 1 8 2014		